To Abe and Janice
with fond wishes -
    Cornelia (Schmalz-Jacobsen)
      Maplewood
        Oct. 14th 2015

Other Publications from Humanity in Action Press

Transatlantic Perspectives on Diplomacy and Diversity
Anthony Chase, Editor (2015)

Humanity in Action: Collected Essays and Talks
Judith S. Goldstein (2014)

Civil Society and the Holocaust: International Perspectives on Resistance and Rescue
Anders Jerichow and Cecilia Felicia Stokholm Banke, Editors (2013)

Oktober ,43: Danske jøders flugt til Sverige eller deportation til Theresienstad
Anders Jerichow, Editor (2013)

Reflections on the Holocaust
Julia Zarankin, Editor (2011)

Cornelia Schmalz-Jacobsen

Two Trees in Jerusalem

Humanity in Action Press
New York

Funding for the English translation has been generously provided by Neil Karbank in memory of Barney A. and Rose M. Karbank.

Humanity in Action Press

Published in the United States by Humanity in Action, Inc., (New York).

ISBN-10: 0996403000
ISBN-13: 978-0-9964030-0-9

English translation by Margot Bettauer Dembo

Funding for the English translation has been generously provided by Neil Karbank in memory of Barney A. and Rose M. Karbank.

Cover photos:
Eberhard Helmrich's carob tree and
Donata Helmrich's olive tree in Yad Yashem
Eberhard Helmrich, November 1948 and Donata Helmrich, 1946

Unless otherwise indicated, the photos in this book come from the author.

Cover and book design by Friedrich Veitl

Humanity in Action
www.humanityinaction.org

For My Sons
Kai, Jan and Tilo

Foreword

Josef Joffe[1]

Yad Vashem, Jerusalem: On a stiflingly hot April day in 1987, the State of Israel honored a German woman, Donata Helmrich, with a tree in the "Avenue of the Righteous." Donata, who had died in the preceding year, was now one of the "Righteous Gentiles," one out of 525 Germans who had risked their lives to save Jews during the Shoa. Donata's husband Eberhard had been so ennobled 19 years earlier. Their daughter Cornelia, the author of this book and a public figure in Germany, stood in for her mother at the tree-planting ceremony.

Two little girls walked up to her, each with a bouquet of flowers in hand: "Many thanks to your parents for having saved the life of our grandmother." These few words, almost like a well-bred child's polite thank-you note, tell the whole story. It began in Hitler's Germany in the 1940s and ended on this sweltering April day with the presentation of a medallion inscribed with Donata's name and an iconic quote from the Talmud: "Whoever saves one life, saves the whole world" *(Sanhedrin 37a)*.[2]

There weren't many in Nazi Germany who saved one life, let alone many score, as had Cornelia's parents Eberhard and Donata. Just a few more than five-hundred have been honored by Israel. The entire story reads like the original version of *Schindler's List*, the movie made by Steven Spielberg in 1993. Eberhard ran a farm in Drohobicz, a small town in the old Habsburg possession of Galicia. On this plantation, he raised fruit and vegetables for the killers, the Gestapo and the *Sicherheitspolizei* (security

---

1   Editor of *Die Zeit* in Hamburg and Visiting Professor of Political Science at Stanford University

2   The original reads: "Whosoever preserves a single soul of Israel, scripture ascribes merit to him as though he had preserved a complete world."

police). With just a hint of black humor, the author quotes one of the survivors, Leopold Lustig: "There were more workers than tomatoes." Lustig went on to a professorship at Harvard.

The orchard was only officially a farm. In truth, it was a life-saving refuge for several hundred young Jews who would be spared the death camps as long as they were sowing, plucking and reaping. But for how long? Somehow, these "walking dead" would have to be whisked from the grip of the Gestapo. This is where Donata, living in Berlin, came in.

The "pipeline of life" began in Drohobicz and ended in the capital of the Third Reich, some 600 miles to the northwest. Into the pipeline went young Jewish women, out came "Aryan" maids and cleaning women who, after a rest at the Helmrich home in Berlin, were farmed out to German households with false names and papers. Nor was this all. Various branches of the "underground railroad," to use an American term from the Civil War era, led to Hungary and other parts of Poland, carrying young men to safety. Thus, to recall the Talmud, the world was saved two-hundred and fifty times over. Not a bad record for two brave, indeed, heroic people.

Why did the Helmrichs turn into *tsadikim*, the Hebrew term for "the righteous" or "the just?" According to Jewish legend, the world can only persist if in each generation a *tsadik* is born who may not even know that he or she is among the chosen. For the sake of these righteous, the legend continues, God saves the world even if mankind had fallen prey to unregenerate barbarism.

The Helmrichs did not know that they were among the Just and Righteous. Probably, they did not care. They just did what moral duty demanded. "My father decided," recalls daughter Cornelia, "that it would be better for their children to have dead rather than cowardly parents." Mother added: "If the two of us save just two lives, we will be even with Hitler." (In fact, they came out way ahead – with a magnificent return.) How could Donata feed and place these "Aryan" guests of hers? Because among those eighty million Germans, there were other, though nameless Just and Righteous who formed an "invisible root system of helpers." These people knew, but did not betray. What's more, they handed over (strictly rationed) food and took in the escapees whom father Eberhard had snatched from the jaws of certain death.

Cornelia Schmalz-Jacobsen's book is not just about "two trees in Jerusalem," but about their "roots" in Nazi Berlin – about all those ordinary people who did not fall for the demented dream of a *judenrein* Europe, who braved the most horrifying retribution, and who did what decency demanded. "What would I have done?" Cornelia has been asking herself all her adult life. Though this book is a declaration of love to her parents, she avoids phony sentiment and moralizing posturing. She simply answers her own question with sober and modest realism: "I have not been able to answer it."

What would we have done? Especially during the twelve-year Nazi nightmare where "justice," "goodness" or merely "pity" risked Gestapo torture or even death. Only the obtuse or mendacious would crow: "I would have done the right thing." An overwhelming proportion of eighty million Germans did not. This is why *Two Trees in Jerusalem* is so important – never mind that the literature about the Hitlerian horror fills a small library by now.

Donata and Eberhard *did* the right thing. They were heroes in the classical tradition, two people who accomplished "unheard deeds" by putting their own lives on the line. But *Two Trees* is more than a morality tale from hell. The book is also history at its best. It is written from the "bottom up," with ordinary people at the center. It is authored by a trained journalist (and political leader) with a fine eye for colorful detail as well as historical background. What she vaguely saw and heard as a small child, she weaves into a dispassionate, yet soul-touching narrative that is both enlightening and enthralling – a "must read" for anybody who seeks to understand the darkest chapter of human history.

Of course, this story has no happy end. How could it when Nazi Germany almost succeeded in annihilating European Jewry? There weren't enough Schindlers and Helmrichs; the gap between righteousness and mass murder remained a cosmic one. No happy end, but a quantum of solace we shall call "justice and recognition." It comes in the shape of a plaque and two trees in Yad Vashem's Avenue of the Righteous. These symbols shall forever remind the world of two *tsadikim* who "saved Jews at the risk of their own lives." And if the Talmud is right, they also saved the entire world.

1

A man hands me a small, green sapling across the edge of the planting bed in which I stand. I carefully remove the plastic wrapper from the root ball, gently put it into the prepared soil, and tamp the soil down around it. There are already other little trees growing in the narrow strip of land, each with a small name plaque on the ground in front of it. Someone hands me a pail of water so that I can sprinkle some on the little tree. With a second pail of water, Tilo, my fifteen-year-old son, waters the tiny olive tree that is no more than a thin twig. At this moment I hope with all my heart that it will grow and thrive, that one day it will provide shade and fruit. I am thinking of the woman this tree is intended to memorialize – my mother, Donata. It is in her honor that so many people – there may be forty – have gathered here in this place. I am aware of them, but I can't make out their faces just now. It is all blurry, the flight to Tel Aviv, the strict airport inspections, the drive here. I'm all mixed up, and it's so hot this April day in the year 1987. I'd very much like to take off my dark jacket.

This is Yad Vashem. It is situated at the edge of Jerusalem. From the knoll on which we're standing one can see far across the hills of Judea into a Biblical landscape. It is peaceful and quiet here in this place, although many young men and women in the uniform of the Israeli Army are noisily talking and laughing at the entrance. The name "Yad Vashem" comes from the Bible. The Hebrew words mean "Memorial." This is the Israeli memorial site to the murdered Jews. The Israeli Parliament legally created it in 1953. The "Avenue of the Righteous" was officially dedicated in May 1963. There, the honorary title of "Righteous among the Nations" is conferred upon non-Jewish rescuers of persecuted

Jews. The "Avenue" is actually a grove in which three different kinds of trees have been planted close together, trees that are typical for the region: St. John's bread or carob trees, olive trees, and Jerusalem pines, almost two thousand, for individuals who were identified as having saved the lives of Jews during the Holocaust. Until a few years ago, when there was no more room. Those rescuers who were discovered only later have been and are still being honored by a name plaque bearing their names placed on one of the memorial walls built near the grove. By the beginning of 2013, 525 German rescuers had been awarded this honor: they have also been honored at the Holocaust Museum in Washington, D.C. where their names are listed on a large panel.

The names on the plaques under the trees at Yad Vashem tell of a small, incredibly courageous contingent of Europeans – of Poles, Ukrainians, Czechs, Frenchmen, Belgians, Dutch, Italians, Germans, Danes and others, who did the most obvious thing by helping people who were in need, before the ever-present fear for their own lives could get the upper hand.

At the time I was at Yad Vashem, Dr. Mordecai Paldiel was the Director of the "Righteous Among the Nations" Department. His signature is on the letter that informed my family of the honor. After the tree planting he leads us into a large rectangular building, really a large hall with not much light. The ceremony that takes place there is both impressive and depressing. One small flame burns in the dim room, and my son and I are shown how to make it flare up with the help of an iron lever. We try hard to do it right. The flame shoots up into the room – the symbolism is inescapable and compelling: Hope must never die!

After the ceremony we are presented with a document and a little wooden box. Inside is a medallion inscribed with my mother's name. *"Quiconque sauve une vie sauve l'univers tout entier"* (Whoever saves one life, saves the entire world) – This line from the Talmud is engraved on it in French because in 1963, when they first started presenting these awards, French was the official second language in Israel.

The short path across the dusty yellow sand to the Memorial Hall seemed very long to me. In reality it couldn't have been more than a five-minute walk. On the way we pass other trees, and I try to read the name plaques. "Eberhard Helmrich, Germany" it says on one, a large carob tree – it is the memorial tree for my father. There is a special story behind the fact that a married couple was honored here, yet not at the same time and with not just one tree but with two, and that nineteen years passed between the two ceremonies.

My father was able to plant his own tree in March 1968, one year before his death. He came here for this purpose from New York, where he had emigrated in 1949. My mother survived him by seventeen years. She was informed of the plans to award her the honor, but was not able to accept it in person. We planted the little olive tree for her shortly after the first anniversary of her death on Holocaust Memorial Day in 1987. The plaque under my family's second tree on the "Avenue of the Righteous" reads: "Donata Helmrich, Germany." The two trees are less than thirty yards apart.

My mother had rather mixed feelings about honors like this. She even used to laugh a little about them, "Since when do they honor people for behaving normally?" In her eyes it was the others who weren't normal – the barbarians, the murderers, the informers, and the collaborators.

After the ceremony in the stifling hot room, Dr. Paldiel takes us to a high-ceilinged, paneled room for a kind of press conference for which I'm not properly prepared. I speak about my parents, how I felt about them as a little girl. I tell the assembled reporters what my older brother and sisters, my parents' friends, and my mother later told me about the things that happened. And I try to explain that back then you couldn't save anyone without other helpers. People who were in the know, or others who only suspected what was going on but who kept silent about it. I tell them about people who made a bed available for a few nights, and about those who stuffed a few extra potatoes, an additional two pounds of fish into my mother's shopping bag, or who donated a warm sweater. During the war, if you got things from "under the counter," that meant it wasn't quite legal.

After the press conference, Tilo and I are invited by our escorts to have lunch in a restaurant in the city. It is quite festive. We are assigned seats on a sort of stage with the then-German Ambassador, Dr. Wilhelm Haas, and an Israeli man and his young son. Not until we're inside the restaurant do I really see the individual people and greet them. Two girls come up to me; they are about eight and nine years old, and each hands me a small bouquet of flowers and saying, "Many thanks to your parents for having saved the life of our grandmother." They say it like good little girls, as if it were an ordinary "Thanks for the invitation." An older woman tells me that she had lived with us in our home on Westend Allee in Berlin with fake documents and had later emigrated to Palestine. The Israeli sitting next to me, a man about my age, recounts the story of his father who, at some risk, was turned into an "Aryan" and, together with my father, protected, concealed, and saved people during those horrible years under the so-called *Generalgouvernement* in Poland in the 1940's. I was familiar with his father's name; it was Naftali Backenroth, "the engineer." Later he had dropped that name and chosen the name "Bronicki" for himself and all the surviving members of his family – a name with a sinister connotation, which I shall explain later.

Everyone there had a story to tell, their own or that of relatives or friends. Stories that left one speechless. I found it hard to say anything. After all, I wasn't the rescuer, the one who had rescued them. Although I must say that all my life I have asked myself the question, "What would you have done?" – yet have not been able to answer it.

The story of those "ordinary" citizens, the civilians, who were helpers in Germany – in both parts of Germany, East and West – has never been fully recognized.

Perhaps it would be more to the point to say that the Germans have driven it from their collective consciousness. One exception is Oskar Schindler, popularized by Steven Spielberg's film *Schindler's List*. Twenty-five years after the end of the war, the government of the Federal Republic made a start at finding German rescuers. Without any real awareness on the part of the public, it awarded the *Bundesverdienstkreuz* to about two hundred individuals. But then only a few years later, the Government gave up playing an active role in the search for other helpers. Since then it acts only on very specific leads by third parties. Not until a few years ago, rather belatedly, has any thorough research on this subject begun.

The myth that there was no third way, no alternative to obedience or death, has held sway over the decades. It is convenient and comforting for the collaborators and those who looked away to hold on to the conviction that although there may have been a small minority of heroes and martyrs, they all had to pay with their lives. Every year we commemorate the men of July 20th, and we remember with horror the young and utterly fearless students of the "White Rose." We name schools in their honor and admire their uprightness – and rightly so.

However, those others who risked resisting in their quite normal, everyday lives, present a challenge, even a humiliation to all those who steadfastly claimed that there was no possibility of making a choice under the terror of the Nazi Dictatorship. Yet it seemed that during that regime of violence and informers there was a small percentage of citizens who *did* make the choice, who were immune to the lie, the baiting, and threats. They acted like the yeast of a civil society.

What sort of people are these whose ethical and moral

systems remain intact, and who stand incorruptible, who know even in borderline situations what is right and what is wrong, and who have the courage to act accordingly?

2

My mother was as old as the last century – She was born in 1900. When I think of her, I see various pictures and events in a series of dissolves. As the young woman with thick, black hair that I loved to make into braids that she hated. As the mother who rarely had time for me, but when I was sick would conjure up a heavenly atmosphere of happiness with her care and endless spoiling. As the careworn woman in the postwar days, who laughingly called herself *"Trockenobstchen"* (Little dried fruit). Not much later she became a successful conference interpreter, much in demand on the international scene. It was a career she started at the age of fifty and which lasted almost until her eightieth birthday.

It suited her: the many trips abroad, the international setting that she had missed so much during the Nazi years, always new subjects and perspectives that she handled with élan and determination. Coming home from her trips, she would describe for us in glowing colors the encounters with various people and fields of knowledge. It was probably the happiest period of her life. At the same time I can also see her in her other life as the devoted "Ama," grandmother to my children, in her little house, her refuge, on the isle of Sylt—"Grandchild Central," as she called it.

She was vivacious, empathetic, quick in thought and action, confusingly inconsistent in bringing us up – sometimes strict and demanding, sometimes indifferent and uninterested. She was extremely competent and hard-working and incredibly courageous. Her predominant qualities were, it seems to me, her talent never to let anyone put anything over on her, and her amazing generosity and goodness.

Donata was the child of an unusual marriage. Her mother came from an upper middle-class Greek family; her father, Ernst Hardt, was by comparison quite poor; his father had been a Prussian army officer, a career that he had also envisioned for his son, my grandfather. But he, at the age of sixteen, ran away from the cadet corps, preferring to occupy himself with copying manuscripts, tutoring French, and similar things, so as to be able to follow his literary inclination. When he met his future wife in Athens, he was a penniless young German writer and journalist, not exactly one's dream of a son-in-law. But the young woman finally had her way; all efforts to interfere with their *amour fou* failed.

The young family spent their first years with Donata's grandparents in Athens. Then they moved to Weimar. There the young writer Ernst Hardt suddenly scored a big success with his plays. In 1908 he was awarded the Schiller Prize and the Prussian State Prize for his play, *Tantris der Narr* (Tantris, the Fool). And suddenly the family's life was on a more solid footing. They moved into a beautiful house "On the Horn," and my mother and her five-year-younger brother grew up in an atmosphere filled with cultural stimulation and intellectual liberalism.

Hardt was appointed Director of the historic Weimar National Theater in 1919. As director of the theater and a passionate democrat he welcomed the National Assembly. For the occasion he staged *William Tell* and composed an ode in which the dawn of a new day foretold better days. By today's standards it would be considered rather pompous.

Donata's mother, Polyxeni, had studied art history in her native city – which was unusual for women in those days – and expected her daughter to get a professional education as well. And so Donata was sent, against her will, to a women's vocational college and passed the examination as a teacher of English and French.

Once the children had grown up, the parents separated. Polyxeni moved with her son Prosper to Berlin, not far from where Donata was living. Her father moved to Cologne in 1926, having been appointed Director of the newly founded West German Radio (*Rundfunk*) by the mayor of Cologne at that time, Konrad Adenauer. Her mother, my grandmother "Zazi," started a quite successful career as an art dealer at this point in her life.

Donata married when she was twenty-two, and shortly thereafter had three children – my two half-sisters and half-brother. We always thought of ourselves as "real" siblings since we grew up in the same household with our mother. Her first marriage did not last long, and so Donata raised her three children alone. She supported herself and her children as a secretary and translator, with help from her mother.

In 1931 my mother met my father. Eberhard Helmrich came from a strict and perhaps arrogant Hamburg family of businessmen. I never got to know my grandparents since they did not at all approve of their son's marriage to a "divorcee" with three children. They rejected us out of hand. I never missed them.

Eberhard did not follow in the family tradition; he did not become a businessman, but instead studied agriculture in Munich. His family did not give him much money, and he earned his living by, among other things, accompanying transports of cattle and grain. He traveled to international agricultural shows, going as far as South America. There is a silver cigarette case he brought back from that trip. On the outside it is engraved with the puzzling inscription, "Eberhard Helmrich, from his grateful potatoes." It was a present from the men who were working for him. Many of those who knew him well said that he always had a special talent for dealing with people.

I remember my father as a quiet man with a gentle smile and a soft voice that actually didn't fit his physical appearance. As a little girl I didn't realize that, of course. He was very tall, 6 feet 4 inches – a giant, gentle man with an amazing amount of natural authority and the courage of a lion, as it later turned out.

My parents were married on April 1, 1933. There was to be a happy family celebration at the elegant Café Kranzler on Unter den Linden in Berlin. A big event, indeed, for "going out" was not an everyday thing for us. The family lived modestly. My siblings remember that for weeks beforehand they were very excited about it – probably less because of the wedding itself than because of the party at the elegant, fashionable "Kranzler" afterward – and because they had been warned at home beforehand how they were to behave and what not to do. "You can't go to the Kranzler if you're going to be messy," they were threatened.

And then suddenly, to the children's great disappointment, the beautiful celebration was canceled. Their parents had decided to stay at home.

It was the day of the first *Judenaktion*; the National Socialist government had staged an anti-Jewish boycott. All over the German Reich, SA formations stood guard outside shops, stores, and lawyers' and doctors' offices owned by Jews with warning placards to keep the public from entering them. In various places they photographed people who shopped or entered the stores. In the evening, movie theaters owned by Jews were "boycotted." All this happened not only in busy commercial neighborhoods but also at smaller Jewish businesses where the SA vilified people and smeared shop windows with anti-Jewish slogans. That afternoon, at an organized rally Joseph Goebbels, the Gauleiter of Berlin-Brandenburg and Reich Minister for Propaganda, spoke about the next measures to be taken against the Jews.

So instead of going to the Kranzler, the family went to Grandmother Zazi's. "We always thought it would peter out," my mother said, "that it would take its course and go away like the measles or chickenpox." It was a miscalculation to which many succumbed. It didn't go away – it was all just beginning.

20

Eberhard and Donata Helmrich, in the early 1930s

Donata Helmrich, in the 1930s

Eberhard Helmrich and the three siblings, in the 1930s

Summer 1936 on the Island of Sylt,
the three siblings

3

The Helmriches lived in the far western part of the Charlottenburg district, in Neuwestend, in a row house on Westend Allee near the Reich Sports Field which was just then under construction and where the 1936 Olympics would be held. Neuwestend, even today, is a pleasant, friendly area with a lot of greenery, shady avenues, some nice places where children can play, old people can sit on benches, and couples can smooch. Tuesdays and Fridays, as long as I can remember, there was a market on Preussen Allee, and on the upscale Reichsstrasse in Westend where you could buy whatever you needed. This district was never as classy as Dahlem or Grunewald, but it always retained a little of its village character. One could live well there without being subjected to the tumult of the big city.

Our family led an unspectacular life. During the week Eberhard was usually traveling in the Uckermark, the outskirts of Berlin, on estates whose owners were in financial difficulties. It was his job, with the help of the owners, to get the estates or farms up and running again, to make them prosper. Even though from the owners' point of view this couldn't have been an exactly popular activity, he developed friendships with a few of the families. Some of these proved to be useful and worthwhile during the most difficult times of the dictatorship and lasted to the end of World War II. Two of the friendships even for longer.

Donata was a housewife and added to the family income by doing translation work. My three siblings – two sisters and one brother – who were eight to twelve years older than I was went to Miss Wolf's private school until they started high school. The three of them, in contrast to me, had a very sheltered pre-war childhood with lots of activities, children's birthdays, excursions to the country, and even piano lessons for the eldest. They spent the summer vacation at the Baltic Sea. Yet it would have been totally wrong to think of Donata as a mousy little homebody standing over a hot stove. She was lively and full of joy, and loved being surrounded by "life." For her that meant: lots of people, the more the better, and the more varied they were, the more exciting it was for her. She took pleasure in keeping an open house, even if her husband sometimes felt it was too much for him. He kidded her about her "Inn at the Patient Lamb," but on the whole he rather enjoyed this contrast to his own calm nature – the lively discussions, the laughter, the large company at mealtimes, the music-making.

Unless they had Jewish friends or knew individuals considered questionable by the National Socialists, many of the people living in Westend and the other outer districts of the city may not have noticed the drastic changes that the year 1933 brought. The new regime had obviously prepared beforehand to take control: The flood of laws and regulations promulgated just that first year seems to us today incomprehensible. The new rulers did not waste any time. They started quickly with the first harassment of Jews and prohibiting Jewish doctors, lawyers, and teachers to practice their professions. Men who had fought on the front lines in the First World War were, for the time being at least, exempt from these rulings. There were restrictions for Jewish-owned businesses and special regulations for Jewish individuals living on welfare. In mid-August 1933, Jews were prohibited from swimming at the Wannsee beach, and in October the Grunewald Rotweiss Tennis Club expelled its "non-Aryan" members. Four weeks later it also expelled those married to non-Aryans. The screw was beginning to turn alarmingly fast; yet there were many opponents to the new regime who could not or did not want to think that there might be much worse to come. On the contrary, even among those directly affected, the Jews, there were many who thought these developments were all just a transitional nuisance; they felt certain that common sense and normality would soon return.

The Helmrich family felt the impact almost immediately: Donata's father was dismissed as Director of West German Radio and sent to "Klingelpütz," the Cologne prison.

Ironic though it may sound, Ernst Hardt, the Social Democrat, and Joseph Goebbels, the National Socialist, had one thing in common: They both took the role of radio as a public medium seriously. But an independent spirit like 50-year-old Hardt was profoundly opposed to the ideals of the propagandists. As director he had managed to turn a slapstick radio station once viewed with deprecatory disapproval by many intellectuals in the fields of science and culture into a successful and popular, cultural institution.

His primary consideration relating to the program schedule was: "What do people need?" Enthusiastically he threw himself into his new assignment. He experimented with radio plays. For the first time stage plays were adapted for radio. The "actors dressed for these live broadcasts as if they were going to the theater," according to a later description of those times. Georg Büchner's *Woyzeck*, plays by Bertolt Brecht and many other writers were presented to a wide listening audience.

There were radio concerts on a regular basis; the first radio broadcasts to schools were sent out over the airwaves. After the first broadcast of a soccer game, the station received 25,000 letters from listeners. A weekly program called "*Die Stunde des Arbeiters*" (The Worker's Hour) must also have had a large audience, for the pieces that were mailed in to the station provided material for a follow up series called "Unpublished Writers." Ernst Hardt had an ambitious goal: quality programming for a broad populace of all levels – "achieving knowledge and understanding of the world by means of teaching and education" was how he expressed it.

Political commentary, which today is the pillar of every station's political department, was still new territory when it was introduced on the daily magazine program "*Vom Tage*" (Today) in 1928. It also proved very successful. It is easy to imagine the idealism and enthusiasm – and the hard work – with which these radio "producers" intended to structure the new medium in accordance with their ideas. There are brief statements relating to that time in the Archive of the West German Rundfunk, such as "minimal influence on the part of the programming advisory board." But the feedback from listeners grew from month to month. No wonder that Goebbels displayed a very special interest in this broadcast station.

Ernst Hardt's first interrogation by the Gestapo took place in the spring of 1933. Perhaps they thought they'd be able to win the well-known broadcaster over to their goals, but if it really was an attempt on the part of the Nazis to get him to work on their behalf, it failed utterly. The answer my grandfather gave them at the interrogation is on the record: "I have always been social and national, but I never had the hyphen,[3] and I never shall," was his curt answer. As to the unfair demand that he fire his Jewish coworkers and staff, his reaction was unequivocal – he refused. A short time later, after further urging to "cleanse" the broadcast center of Jewish employees and his renewed refusal to do so, and before he himself could be fired, he submitted his "voluntary" resignation, which the powers-that-be accepted instantly.

Yet he didn't quite trust the peaceful calm that ensued, and he was proved right. Although the new masters had assured him they would continue to pay his salary until his contract ran out, he was fired four weeks later – retrospectively – without notice. Thus his contract was no longer in effect, and he was banned from the premises. This was followed by house searches, and an

---

3   This referred to the way the name of the Nazi Party was written in German "Nazional-Sozialistische Partei."

overzealous public prosecutor who probably wanted to further his national-socialist career, brought charges against him on some flimsy political grounds. Hardt moved from his beautiful house at the edge of Bergisches Land (Land of Berg) to prison. He became ill there and found refuge at the St. Anna Hospital in Cologne. The case against him was suspended on the grounds of illness, and was dropped three years later without any fuss. It had been an extraordinarily foolish abuse of power even for the Nazis' customary practices.

Nevertheless, the ruling laid down by the "*Reichsschrifttumskammer*" (Reich Cultural Chamber) and the order issued to publishers, librarians, and bookstores remained in effect a full twelve years thereafter: a ban on the publication of any works by Ernst Hardt. Not a line written by Ernst Hardt, or even anything translated by him was permitted to be printed or reprinted in the German Reich. He was treated as if he didn't exist and during the years that followed, he lived a life on the sidelines although still in the capital, for he had moved to Berlin Westend, not far from his daughter Donata and her family. There he lived alone with his tomcat Gustav in a small apartment on the Preussen Allee. He had nothing left of the things he had been accustomed to during his twenty-five years of prosperity. And his passion for extravagant, fast cars especially was once and for all relegated to the past. He was poor once more. He gradually sold off his belongings, piece by piece. Now and then he could get a literary translation published in a journal under the pseudonym "Alexander Vult." Then, in 1938 something quite surprising happened: The wife of Reichsmarshall Göring, the former actress Emmy Sonnemann, arranged for a small but regular pension for him.

I remember him as a strict, handsome, elderly gentleman, who remained a stranger to me even though he was my grandfather. He was always impeccably dressed – in the winter he wore an overcoat with a fur collar, in the summer, a light-colored linen jacket. During that period he often came to our house for lunch, and I remember that he laid great emphasis on our having good table manners and speaking "proper German." We were always admonished to pay attention to both, especially me, the youngest.

Luckily I have another memory – Opapa, as we called him, could do magic tricks! With his well-cared-for, deft hands he could conjure coins out of one's nose, make objects disappear, and change the pattern on my light-blue-and-white blanket. He would shake it vigorously a couple of times and already the lion in the woven pattern which had always been in the left corner would turn up in the right one, and the zebra from the lower edge would suddenly be at the top edge. I admired this talent of his a lot, and would boast to my girlfriends about my grandfather who was a magician. But he was also a writer; I knew that from my mother. And sometimes, too rarely it seemed to me, he would take the time to tell us wonderful stories. I don't remember exactly what they were about, only that we were no longer sitting in the garden or in our rooms, but rather in enchanting fields, far away by a big sea.

My sisters and brother don't recall that he ever complained about his fate to his family. But there is no doubt that he suffered more from this exclusion from the intellectual life of his homeland than from any other personal restrictions. In letters to old friends he expresses anger and resignation, but above all bitter criticism of those former coworkers who after 1933 nimbly rushed to fall in line with the "brown columns" and offered their services to them, conforming both inwardly and outwardly.

He spent the last year of the war and twenty months after that in a small village in Bavaria, Ichenhausen on the Günz. He remained to the end an upright, straightforward man. By the end of the war he was quite ill, but he refused to be recognized as a victim of the Third Reich in the way the men and women of the Resistance were. He had certainly been a steadfast opponent of the regime from the beginning, but Resistance? – No, that he hadn't done. From his correspondence of those months it looks as if his former zest for action flared up once more. At the time he wrote small pieces for the Northwest German Rundfunk on a volunteer basis. The time had run out for larger assignments.

He thought a great deal about the medium itself and reflected about its future. In a letter he wrote: "Radio broadcasting really has no greater task at this time and in the immediate future than mustering all the spiritual and intellectual powers available in Germany for the purpose of helping the many lost, poisoned, hardened Nazi minds, to convince them and to inwardly fill them with the desire to return to spiritual and intellectually worthwhile views of justice, law, the state, and personal responsibility before God and humanity."

In March 1946, he managed, with a great deal of effort, to complete the a novel he had been working on for ten years. He sent the manuscript of "*Don Hjalmar*" to his old publisher, Insel Verlag, which published it in early December 1946.

One of Ernst Hardt's last letters was to his publisher, Anton Kippenberg: "What happened the day before yesterday gave me, so to say, my final joy on earth. I woke up and on my blanket lay *Hjalmar* like a pre-war work dating to the best period of the Insel Verlag. I can't speak or write about it without, in my present somewhat fragile nervous state, having the tears come to my voice and my breath."

The reply to his letter arrived too late. Ernst Hardt died January 3, 1947. He was seventy years old.

4

Back again to the early years of the "Third Reich":

Even though Donata's father had been discharged from his position, and in spite of all the annoyances friends of the Helmriches were subjected to, life with all its daily tasks and demands went on rather normally for Donata and Eberhard. They were a young married couple, happy with each other, and their most fervent hope was that it would remain that way.

Some snapshots from that time: On a hike outside Berlin the couple met a truck full of uniformed SA men standing in the truck bed bellowing songs. One could hear them coming from far away. As they passed the couple, all raised their right hands and yelled, "Heil Hitler!" Donata and Eberhard laughed merrily, not thinking of returning the salute. They just waved back pleasantly. Several of the SA people yelled down from the truck: "This is how you give a German greeting," once more raising their right arms and threatening the two. Donata and Eberhard looked at each other in disbelief. "What a stupid greeting," Donata said, shaking her head.

After having walked on silently for a few yards, Donata said, "This can't possibly last – it's all so crazy!" Perhaps they wanted to boost each other's courage in the face of all the signs of the times. Many other people thought so too.

The first Jews in their circle of acquaintances were beginning to wonder whether it wouldn't be better to leave Germany and go to Switzerland or England – at least for the time being. Some, as a precaution, sent their children to study abroad. Yet, among the so-called assimilated Jews who considered themselves an integrated part of the German population, sharing the same language, a common history, and the same hopes for the future, the majority felt that even though it might get worse with more restrictions being imposed, in the end it would all pass. Torture and killings. Deportation and mass murder seemed as yet unthinkable.

In 1934, Donata became pregnant with me, her fourth child. An acquaintance advised her to register with the Health Department, because she had heard that the state would pay the delivery costs for a family's fourth child, as well as an additional allowance of two hundred mark. And since the family wasn't exactly swimming in money just then, Donata thought, "Why not?" She could at least find out more without making any commitments. So she took her questions to the Public Health Department in Charlottenburg, and the conversation with the woman official there went something like this: "Ah yes, Mrs. Helmrich, first I need to know whether this is an extra child for the purposes and as defined by the law."

Donata: "Excuse me, but what is an extra child?"

The official: "An extra child is a child which the parents decided to have solely on the basis of a consultation with the Public Health Department or another office."

Whereupon Donata said, "Aha, then this is probably a misunderstanding. Because in my case this is a child that we wanted to have anyway. Thank you very much. I'm sorry but I'll have to do without the public subsidy." She said it and left. In retelling the story my mother liked to embellish the scene a bit: "A little longer, and the woman would have asked me whether we also – well you know already – whether we are giving the Führer a child," Those were the words of a slogan that the Nazis intended quite seriously, even if it sounds like pure sarcasm.

The "extra child story" tag stuck to me for a long time. My brother and sisters, and sometimes my mother really made me mad, picking on me that way. Even though I knew it was only in fun, it hurt my feelings. My parents had actually "planned" to have another child, but when the right moment came to do it, it seemed that the times were not good for increasing the family size. Even at a very advanced age, my mother still held this against the "Thousand-year Reich."

Later, in 1939, the Nazi state introduced a special medal for mothers with four or more children, whether or not the children were wanted or "extra" – it was called the *Mutterkreuz* (Mother Cross Medal). It looked like a round metal candy that the mothers were supposed to proudly wear on their chests. In our house the thing was tossed into the button box; my mother never wore it. But now and then, in fun, she would lend it to friends who didn't have any children. I remember a female couple who were known all along the avenue – one partner was slender, elegant, and aristocratic in her man's suit; the other was jolly, bosomy, with big bulging eyes. One of them was wearing my mother's "Mother Medal" pinned to her blouse as they were proudly walking arm in arm through the market on Preussen Allee....

As the months passed, the question of emigrating or not took on more significance. And not only in Jewish families, but also at official places, though it may sound strange today. It's hard to call them "lawmakers or legislators" in this context in view of the arbitrariness and injustice – but it clearly states in the relevant announcements about the "Jewish Question" of 1933, and later as well, that – these were the actual words – "the emigration of Jews is desired." On the other hand, the Nazis also worried about the resulting loss in tax receipts. In 1931, during a difficult economic period, Reich Chancelor Brüning introduced the "Reichsfluchtsteuer" (a tax on those fleeing from the Reich), so as to put a brake on the flight of capital out of Germany. After 1933, the National Socialists used this legal instrument for their own perfidious goals. The state shamelessly grabbed more and more assets: in 1934 the tax exemption limit was still set at two hundred thousand Reichsmark; in 1937 only fifty thousand Mark were excempt from this tax. But shortly after *Kristallnacht*, the Night of Broken Glass, when the *Judenvermögensabgabe* was passed on November 1938, even the small savers became poor as beggars. According to this regulation, all German Jews having savings of at least five thousand Mark had to hand over twenty percent to the Tax Office; later it became twenty-five percent. This merciless plunder of its Jewish citizens netted the German treasury 1.13 billion Reichsmark. Later they dropped these pseudo-legal measures entirely, and Jews who got out of Germany with nothing but their lives could thank their Creator.

The Nazis were intent on grabbing as much material wealth and assets as possible and keeping it. In a decree from that period it says: "To prevent the transfer of assets abroad by Jews, the taking of valuables abroad must be stopped." This was a time of bribery and desperation sales at giveaway prices, just to get the necessary official stamps so that one could leave the country, and it was also the hour of the smuggler – both selfless ones and those driven by profit motives.

My grandmother Zazi – a small, delicate and very elegant woman – went to Holland several times as well as to Switzerland, taking diamonds across the border in her powder box for friends, so it was said. She trusted her sangfroid as well as her Greek passport. But once it did get a bit dangerous. After the customs inspectors – or was it the police? – had examined all the luggage of the travelers, one of them pointed at Zazi's handbag and roughly demanded: "Open up!" My grandmother, it was said, sat bolt upright, flashed an angry look at the inspectors, and in a voice shaking with anger said, "But gentlemen, a lady's pocketbook?!" Whereupon they clicked their heels, laid their fingers to their caps in salute, and with an embarrassed, "Excuse us, Madam," left the compartment.

Donata also occasionally acted as a jewelry smuggler. Of course she was a completely different type than her mother and worked out a different procedure for her trips abroad. It seems she dressed up like a circus horse, openly putting on as much jewelry as she could – hanging it around her neck or pinning it on, and the rest she just put in her luggage.

When a horrified friend asked her, "And what would you have done if they'd come and led you off for questioning?" Donata shrugged and said, "Then I would have pretended that they'd hurt my feelings and said, 'Really, I just like wearing every piece of jewelry I own and like any time I want to! – after all, I'm the Queen of Sheba!'"

"And what if they'd simply taken the jewelry away from you?" It was one of the things one had to reckon with; it would have been too bad. Luckily the situation where she had to pretend to be the Queen of Sheba never came up. Maybe it wouldn't have gone quite so smoothly as she imagined. Without a certain degree of reckless daring all efforts to save herself would not have been possible or practicable. Many times you didn't even try to imagine all the dangers. "Why after all? You always had to make deals and improvise." If you were too afraid of taking a risk – and she was absolutely certain of this – then you shouldn't get involved in the first place, "because that's when it usually goes wrong."

5

It seems that Eberhard wasn't exactly happy in his job rehabilitating farms and estates. Perhaps he didn't like the constant traveling; on the other hand, it may have stimulated him to try something new.

He had two offers that couldn't have been more different from each other. Both came about through Jewish acquaintances. In 1935 Isidor G., a grain dealer, held out an attractive prospect of becoming a successful businessman to my father who apparently liked the idea. Together they founded a company intended to deal in agricultural products on a grand scale. Since neither of them had the means to start up an enterprise of that scale, they had to obtain the required capital from a bank. Donata was totally against this and begged her husband to give up the project. "You may understand a lot about farming, but you don't know anything about business – don't get involved, leave it alone!"

But he turned a deaf ear to her warnings. "You're not usually so fearful of taking risks!"

And so the two men set to work. They were granted a loan; Eberhard guaranteed the loan. As part of the deal, they sold their good little DKW and acquired a more suitable green Ford, to impress potential customers.

Then came the rude awakening; the consequences were to affect our family for a long time afterward. Shortly after the loan was transferred to the joint business account and entered on the books – it's no longer possible to establish just how much money was involved – the money vanished, as did Isidor G. The Helmriches were left with the debts, which they had to pay off over the succeeding years. Now every penny had to be counted. Donata did translations and took on paperwork and writing tasks;

she worked like crazy. As a rule she completed all this additional work "before the family got up," that is to say, before we children woke up in the morning. All she said about it was, "It's a good thing I'm used to getting up early."

Were there arguments about the failed venture? Did she reproach her husband for his foolish deal? I was less than a year old back then, so I don't know. But from what I know of my mother, she probably exploded at first, making an ear-splitting racket, which my father – as I imagine it – just patiently endured in guilty silence. And then, with a kind of grim fury, she resigned herself to the inevitable, rolled up her sleeves, and went to work.

Did this experience affect her willingness to help people? Apparently not in the slightest, surprising though it may seem. I still remember something my father said, "There are decent people everywhere, and there are swindlers everywhere, and that has nothing to do with whether they're Christians, Jews, or something else. Character is character, and a swine is a swine." My mother shared this view of things completely. Needless to say, after this she had an intense allergic reaction to the word "personal guarantee." And "Never guarantee a loan – better to give a gift!" became one of her hard and fast rules. And for decades thereafter "Isidor" remained a sinister synonym for foolishness and financial disaster.

The second offer came a few months after father's unsuccessful attempt to launch a new business career. And it was a completely different sort of thing. One day a well-to-do farmer who had run a sheep farm in Pomerania and whom Eberhard knew through work got in touch with him from England. After the Nazis took control in Germany, this man, whose name I don't know, had acted immediately. He sold his property early enough so that he could get sufficient money for it with which to buy a farm in England, where he had emigrated and settled. He began to raise sheep again. His business was doing very well, and he had decided to enlarge it. So he proposed to Eberhard that he come to England with his family, settle there, and work for him. He had great faith in my father as a farmer and as a man, and he was hoping to have a decision from him as soon as possible.

To get out of Nazi Germany! What a temptation that must have been. In a conversation I taped with my mother in the early nineteen-eighties, she recalls, "Just imagine it, a good job for Eberhard – and well paid. And living in the country on a farm. And in England. English schools for the children. Hard to imagine. Yes indeed, we were sorely tempted." And she continues, "Then a few friends said, 'And what's going to happen to us once you're not here anymore?' So, after thinking it over for a long time, we said to each other, we're not in danger; and in the meantime our name has gotten around, and people know that they can come to us when something goes wrong. We're a little like an Aid Station. And so we deliberately turned down the offer from England. Although with very heavy hearts."

On re-reading this, I wondered whether it wasn't all too good to be true, whether so much altruism is really possible, and if, in looking back, the story wasn't improved on a bit. But who really knows? It would certainly be understandable if other considerations had entered into my parents' final decision. To leave everything behind – it would have been different had they been forced to do so – the beautiful house, their accustomed lives, their friends, a familiar language, and to embark on such an adventure – making a radical new beginning in a not-quite-strange but still somewhat unfamiliar country, and with four children? And would it have turned out well? The dramatic decision to turn your back on your native land, to cut your roots – this is part of every migration story, in every country and all times. So there may very well have been some other good reasons to turn down the tempting offer from England. At any rate, the Helmriches stayed in Berlin.

6

Meanwhile, my parents continued to offer help where needed. Once they kept a suitcase for a few days until someone came to pick it up; another time some rolled-up paintings and gold and silver jewelry were taken abroad and handed over to a trusted person to deposit for the original owners; and they helped friends when they were emigrating.

In the early years it was relatively easy to help those being persecuted by the regime, both Helmriches said. You continued going to the same doctors you'd always gone to, although, if they were Jewish doctors, you had to pay them out of your own pocket because the health insurance no longer would pay them. And so our old pediatrician, Dr. Lissauer, continued to take care of us until he emigrated. (One of his pronouncements remained a saying in our household for years afterward: "One can deal with the children's illnesses – but dealing with the stupidity of the parents…") As the opportunities for Jews to earn money were more and more restricted, "one" deliberately tried to employ Jewish workers. "One"? "Any decent person could do that, and many did," my mother wrote in 1946 for the de-Nazification process of one of my sisters' music teachers. ("PG – but decent." – PG stands for *Parteigenossin*, Party member.) Were there really many? We are more familiar with examples of people who would no longer greet a doctor who had treated them for years when they passed him on the street. So, I ask again, many? Today there is no need to discuss the far-too-many who were enthusiastic about Hitler. Yet gradually we are also beginning to become aware of those who were not mentioned in the written history of the 1930s and 40s. And there were many more of those than is commonly known. There was an invisible network of helpers without which the saving of human lives would not have been possible. A circle of kindred spirits was essential for this in the truest sense of the word.

A little later it could be applied to the help and support that "any decent person" would be willing to give, that is to go shopping for Jewish friends and acquaintances who were no longer allowed to shop at all hours of the day or in all stores. Or just to continue socializing or associating with them as one had before 1933. "No one could come into my living room whom I didn't like. There I'm the one who decides!" Donata would say. It sounded like an incantation.

A date that would drastically alter the lives of Jews and of Jews living together with non-Jews was September 15, 1935. This was the day the infamous Nuremberg Laws were put into effect, which codified the "racial" exclusion of Jews on the part of the State. The "Reich Citizenship Law" gave Jews second class status under the law; they were German subjects but not Reich citizens. Only the latter had full political rights. The "Blutschutz" (Protection of Racial Purity) Law forbade marriages and extra-marital sexual relationships between Jews and non-Jews.

In the months and years that followed, the lives of Jews, euphemistically described as state subjects, became more and more restricted. Through various decrees of the Reich Citizen Law: They were stripped of all rights and subjected to hardships and persecution. The term "Jew" was defined as: "A Jew is someone who is descended from at least three racially full-Jewish grandparents."

In my parents' house the Nuremberg Laws had one unexpected effect. We suddenly acquired a new family member in the person of "Miss Hedda." At the time we had no idea how close and above all how enduring our relationship with her would turn out to be.

7

Once again various things coincided. My brother, following a several-months-long illness, had to spend some time in a sanatorium in the mountains. He was only eleven and too young to cope with his homesickness by himself. And so our mother decided to stay with him for a little while to make life easier for him. There was only one problem: what to do with the youngest child, Cornelia, who was less than a year old.

While my parents were pondering this problem, an acquaintance of my mother's came and asked her whether she could use a reliable woman with experience in taking care of children. The woman was in urgent need of a job, but under no circumstances would she work for a Nazi family. And this was "Fräulein Hedda."

For more than twenty years she had worked in the home of a respected lawyer and notary, Dr. Leopold Samolewitz. She had helped raise his two sons, Kurt and Hans-Werner. Hedda herself had left school when she was fifteen. She had come from Görlitz to the big city of Berlin, and her first job had been as a maid. Her talent with children only came to the fore later on. She was hired by this upper middle class Jewish lawyer and his wife in 1915, a few months before the birth of the second Samolewitz son. They lived on Bayreuther Strasse in the western section of Berlin. Hedda liked it there. She admired the father, probably idolized him a bit. But she didn't admire the artistic mother quite as much; respected her instead. The sons she loved unreservedly. She called them "my boys" as long as she lived. Hedda never had children of her own, and she never married. Even though her employers repeatedly encouraged her to go out to meet people. "You won't find a husband on Hans-Werner's changing table," they would tell her. But the "changing table" and all the things that went with it must have meant more to her than all the dance halls and popular bars.

The Nuremberg Racial Laws brought about an abrupt end to this harmonious relationship with her employers. For according to these laws, female "Aryan" persons under the age of fifty were not permitted to live in a Jewish household in which there was a man. The state was intent on avoiding any possibility of "racial defilement."

And that was how Hedda Rathsack came to the Helmriches. She didn't want to tie herself down to a permanent position right away, though, and insisted that for the time being she just help out temporarily. Oddly enough this temporary status was never expressly changed. Over the years we would occasionally use the appellation to tease our "temporary Hedda," but no contract was ever signed and this status continued until her death in 1975. Until the end she remained loyal to our family and we to her. She got to know my sons and to love them as much as they loved her. It was a special happiness for the elderly woman, for she much preferred boys to girls. Tough luck for me.

The fact that Hedda refused to work for a Nazi family, of course, fit in very well with her new environment. It would have been just as impossible for my parents to take someone into their home who might have disapproved or even betrayed their views and activities as it would have been for Hedda to put up with living with an anti-Semitic family, after her happy life with the Samolewitzes.

The Nazi plans for the 9th of November 1938 were formulated in absolute secrecy. Yet some information must have seeped through. For the doorman of the house where the Samolewitzes lived had warned them. He told them "something bigger" was being planned against the Jews. He had gathered as much from a conversation he had overheard between two travelers while he was at his second job as porter at the Zoo train station. The Helmriches had also heard some vague hints of an imminent "operation." But exactly what was going to happen only those on the "inside" knew. In any case, on November 8th, a day before the infamous *Kristallnacht*, Eberhard called the Samolewitzes. They had been only casual acquaintances, but from Hedda's descriptions he'd gotten to know them better. He urged them to "Pack a little suitcase and come over to our house – don't ask any more questions now; I'll explain when you get here." His voice must have sounded quite urgent, for only a little later the couple arrived at the front door of our house on Westend Allee. They stayed for several days. At that time both their sons were already abroad. A Dr. Rosenfeld also came to take shelter at the Hemriches', thereby avoiding deportation to the Sachsenhausen Concentration Camp. (Later Dr. Rosenfeld managed to emigrate to Buenos Aires; that's all I know about him.)

My mother was always happy about the "elastic walls" of her house, which seemed to get roomier as the need arose. It was actually just a modest row house – from the street it looked as if it had three stories, but seen diagonally, from the garden in back, it had an additional story. There were also two little rooms in the partially finished attic that could only be detected from the garden side of the house.

The National Socialist propaganda called *Kristallnacht* an outburst of "spontaneous popular anger," but in reality it was an organized nation-wide anti-Jewish Pogrom. During night of horror Jewish homes, businesses, and houses of prayer all over Germany were destroyed and plundered, and more than a hundred people were murdered. In Berlin, SA troops and members of the Hitler Youth created especially horrendous destruction in the business neighborhoods on Kurfuerstendamm, Unter den Linden, and Potsdamer Strasse. The people of Berlin took part in the plunder. Synagogues were torched, Jewish establishments like the Poliklinik of the Jewish Community at the Alexander Platz and the school on Choriner Strasse were totally demolished. In the capital city during that long night of terror and shame twelve thousand Jewish men were arrested. Some of them, especially the elderly, died of heart attacks or the consequences of the mistreatment they suffered before being transported to the Sachsenhausen Concentration Camp. Others died in the concentration camp, and many of those who were released a few weeks later, were so sick or so seriously wounded, they had to be taken to the Jewish Hospital for treatment.

Kristallnacht also marked a turning point in the lives of my parents. This was the first time, as far as I know, that people whose lives were in danger found refuge and shelter in our home. Helping the persecuted, or as seen from another perspective, active opposition to the regime and the prevailing ideology had reached a new dimension.

During those weeks Donata and Eberhard came to realize that it was time to make a fundamental, a radical decision. To put it simply: Should they actively continue with their resistance or do nothing and just wait for the end of the "Thousand-year Reich?" For many opponents to the regime, helping condemned and persecuted Jews was the only opportunity for active resistance. Those who had families found themselves in an irreconcilable moral dilemma. The desire to protect persecuted individuals was in direct contradiction to the responsibility for and the wish not to endanger members of their own families. It was impossible to do both at the same time because the one excluded the other. And so my parents had to choose whether they wanted to retain their human decency or risk their own and their children's security.

8

The Samolewitz family escaped getting caught up in the major murder operations. If "good luck" is the opposite of "bad luck," then these four could say they were lucky. But has anyone worried about the painful, profound effects on the lives of this generation (both Jewish and non-Jewish), has anyone imagined the complete upheaval, the collapse of all hopes for the future?

The oldest Samolewitz son, Kurt, had already given up his law studies in 1934 when he was 21 and left Germany to attend hotel vocational schools, first in Switzerland and then England. From there, in 1936, he went to Palestine, to Jerusalem, where he found a job in his chosen field.

Hans-Werner, who was two years younger, was living and working in Czechoslovakia from 1936 on. In 1938, against the express wishes of his parents, he came to Berlin to visit them one last time. In November of that year he went directly from Prague to London.

Many years later, not until 2001, he wrote the story of his parents' lives for his and his brother Kurt's children and grandchildren. Kurt had died by then. The little book begins:

"When Poldi [that was the father's nickname] and his wife had to leave their beloved Germany in 1939, shortly before the start of the Second World War, they left behind them the comfortable life of the German upper middle class. They arrived in Palestine with just ten marks in their pockets. Because my father did everything strictly according to the law, he had never opened a secret bank account in Switzerland, nor did he have access to any other money abroad."

Actually, their father had already started writing the family story in 1956, three years before his death in Jerusalem, where he had been living. Hans-Werner found four notebooks among his father's papers filled with his father's recollections, written in the old-fashioned German script. He translated what there was into English and later wrote the continuation. Leopold Samolewitz had wanted to tell his descendants about the life of his family and others like them in the Germany of the nineteenth and early twentieth century. He wanted them to know a little about these people and their lives in the years before the Nazis willfully put an end to this centuries-long family history. "The people of my generation no longer form a link in the chain of all the generations that received their ideas and ideals from their parents and grandparents, passing them along to the next generation," he wrote. "We are the END, ripped from all that was familiar to us, transplanted into surroundings where, although we had food and a roof over our heads, our home was forever lost to us. A home with familiar memories and all the ties and feelings that define one's homeland. In any case, for people of my age." A little farther on in the text, he writes, "We tried to pass on our values to our children, but they were prevented from experiencing life in the same calm stable environment we had known. They could not build on the tradition we had inherited. They are a new BEGINNING. Perhaps their children will be able to live in an environment where they are protected, where traditions can be passed on. But our descendants will not understand the generations that came before their own parents' generation. They will look back at us as something unfamiliar, as people from another world."

Leopold Samolewitz had been a soldier in the First World War, serving in a Bavarian regiment, and he had always declared himself proud to have defended his Fatherland. He came back from the war with a bullet in his leg that, back then, could not be removed, a troublesome case of asthma, and the "Iron Cross."

He and his wife Else thought it important to lead the life of a modern, enlightened German family. The boys had to engage in a lot of sports, and their father did not like hearing any Yiddish interjected into conversations. His sons went to good schools and were exposed to stimulating people. The family also had a little summer house in Werder on Lake Glindow – that is, until Adolf Hitler took away their German life.

Leopold Samolewitz was 56 years old when he and his wife arrived in Palestine. They moved into a very modest apartment in Tel Aviv. He spoke no Hebrew and only a little English and had to start from scratch. He wanted to be independent, to stand on his own two feet and not be a drain on his son's finances. He worked hard trying to learn the two languages and familiarized himself with the rules of an entirely different legal system so that he could pass the examinations. He succeeded, and in contrast to many other immigrants from Europe, he was finally able to earn his own living again.

In 1946 Kurt married a young woman from Stettin. Rosel had come to Palestine with her thirteen-year-old twin brothers when she was sixteen years old. They had been on a "Youth Aliya" children's transport. "Youth Aliyah" was a Jewish youth organization that saved the lives of thousands of young Jews. Rosel's parents, who had remained behind, were murdered. Kurt and Rosel changed their names right after the founding of the State of Israel. They were now Rachel and Moshe Zamir. Israel became their new homeland. Their children and grandchildren took this all for granted. For them Germany was a foreign country, although one of their daughters did visit Berlin once briefly on a trip through Europe.

Hans-Werner left England after the end of World War II and emigrated to the United States of America. There he married Eva Isaac-Krieger, also in 1946. She had emigrated with her parents from Berlin to New York in 1938. The two families, the

Samolewitzes and the Isaac-Kriegers, had known each other in their "earlier lives" in Germany. Hans-Werner and Eva also changed their names. Hans-Werner used to be called "HaWe"; now he became "Harvey", and "Samolewitz" was shortened to "Samo." Only Eva stayed Eva, although her name was now pronounced the English way. They are first generation Americans. For their children and grandchildren, American citizenship and the "American way of life" are givens, and they can't imagine it any other way. None of them speaks German. Both families, one might add, both the American and the Israeli branch, lead a much more "Jewish" life than their Berlin grandparents had thought appropriate.

The family separation that was forced by the Nazis, caused the various members much sorrow, even though it sounds as if it all had a "Happy Ending." In the twenty-one years between their parting in 1938 and the death of his beloved father, Hans-Werner/Harvey saw his parents only four times. Money was tight, travel was more difficult and more expensive than it is today; there was no e-mail and no fax, and telephoning was complicated and costly. Thus hundreds of air mail letters were what held the family together and kept them closely connected across thousands of miles. Today, almost seventy years later, when the Zamirs and the Samoses say without any hesitation, "We're a fortunate, a lucky family," then it's the comforting, triumphant truth.

9

During those early Nazi years, Donata and Eberhard did not deliberate long; they acted spontaneously. They were neither religious nor particularly politically inclined. Nor did they belong to any established Resistance network – that may have been lucky for them. They simply wanted to be normal in a time when normality "was out to lunch," as my mother would say. Later, both my parents curtly rejected the term "heroes" being applied to them – they had never wanted to be heroes.

But back then, they had to decide whether to go on with what they were doing or to wait for different times. They mulled the question over for about a week, trying to figure out how either decision would affect their children, and what effects it might have on their own lives. When they did finally come to a decision, it was unequivocal: they would continue with what they had been doing.

Later on, Eberhard would even say, "From that moment on, it was easy." They had agreed that they would work hard to do everything they could, that they would have to keep finding new ways, and that they had to make sure their friends were willing to work with them to help "all the people we know." I don't know which one came up with the following sarcastic calculation. I assume it was Donata because it sounds like her grim sense of humor. "If they both had to die, but had saved two lives before their deaths, then they were 'even with Hitler.' Each additional person saved, however, would appear on the credit side of the ledger as "clear profit." What is certain is that they won this private duel with Hitler hands down. Yet they weren't ever able to look at it as a "victory" – too many terrible things they couldn't prevent happened. It weighed heavily on their minds that they didn't do more.

Our parents made no secret of their rejection of *Reich* and *Führer* in front of my siblings, and that's how it was until the German collapse in the spring of 1945. All those years they were in ever more danger. In spite of that they'd say, "Better for our children to have dead parents than cowardly ones." This thought had a sort of liberating effect on Donata and Eberhard; they had left one hurdle behind them.

It certainly wasn't expressed that boldly in front of my siblings, but at their ages – they were between eleven and fifteen at the time – the significance of the parental decision could not have been concealed from them, nor the growing pressure on all dissident thinkers. They must have been worried about their parents, the family, and the future. Yet the trust the Helmriches put in their children made up for a lot. It was a rare gift they gave us. And we treasured it as such all our lives.

Nevertheless, it didn't keep my sister from falling into a deep depression. She knew only too well that we couldn't say anything on the outside about what we thought, talked about, or did in our home. But the day came when she could no longer bear the constant lies and the growing discrepancy between "inside" and "outside." She would come home from school crying uncontrollably and was often sick during those days. My parents took her out of the public girls' high school for a few months and enrolled her in a private school. There she calmed down, and when everything seemed to be going well again, she went back to her old school, from which she graduated in 1941.

Our parents expected a lot from their children – and we were fully aware of it. And because they were convinced that any and all National Socialist influences had to be avoided, and since any compromise was out of the question for them, there could be no secrets within our family. It was agreed that none of us would become members of the NSDAP (Nazi Party), or belong to any of the so-called non-political organizations – which by then were really all conforming with the Nazi ideology. My parents probably lost a lot of sleep worrying that one of their children might be taken in by one of the Nazi groups. Admittedly, the activities of the youth organizations were quite attractive: group hikes and excursions, evening camp fires, sports – lots of nice group experiences. They appealed to young people. And it was exactly this that they had to keep from happening.

In the war year 1939, every fourteen- to eighteen-year-old was legally obligated to become an active member of either the Hitler Youth (HJ) for boys or the League of German Girls (BDM). Younger children between ten and fourteen had to join the *Jungvolk*. Violations could be punished by arrest, fines, and/or penalties for the parents or guardians.

Our parents made it absolutely clear how they felt. "These organizations are not for us; and you're not going to join!" How would that work out? First, we just wait – and then we'd see. My oldest sister remembers the excuse she kept using, "I'm going to be a famous pianist and have to practice – I have no time." A friend in her class who had gotten to be a BDM leader warned her one day that "soon" steps would be taken against "shirkers." Before that could happen, my sister took action. With trembling knees and a cheeky resolve, the seventeen-year-old girl went to the headquarters on Westend Platanen Allee and turned the tables on them. She acted angry and indignant: She had never gotten an invitation to the meetings of the BDM group. What a miserably slipshod way of running things – she felt snubbed, left out. They promised they would look into this embarrassing situation.

When, after a few weeks they actually sent her an invitation to a meeting, she told them she was sorry but that she was now in her last year of high school and was in a class preparing for the final school-leaving exam. And with that she escaped having to join the BDM.

My second sister had rheumatoid arthritis. She was exempt from gym class and could produce a certificate from her doctor to show that she should not be expected to serve in the BDM. Whether this might also have been merely an excuse is something I no longer know today. But in any case, with that she was out of the woods too.

My brother remembers that he really would have liked to participate in those wonderful, exciting hikes, but he wasn't allowed to. There were warnings from the HJ, even threats of punishment, but nothing actually happened to him or our parents.

In April 1946, Donata wrote a statement in which she said with obvious satisfaction, that her children "never participated in any school functions or rallies of the BDM or the Hitler Youth."

A few years before that written statement, when freedom was still far off, the mere knowledge of being on the right side, was not an easy portion for young people.

10

The frequent trips abroad our parents made before war broke out must have been quite unsettling for my brother and sisters. What if they didn't come back?

There was a Jewish family living near us who were friends of my parents, the Sternbergs. I remember that they had two sons who were about ten or eleven and twin daughters who really made an unforgettable impression on four-year-old me at the time. It wasn't only because the girls, who were older than I was and had dark curly hair, were willing to play with me. The special thing about them was that they were alike in all respects and you couldn't tell them apart. Their names were Inge and Marianne, and I decided to call each of them "Ingemanne." If I was referring to both of them, I would say, "Ingemannen" and I'd plead, "Will you come again tomorrow?"

In the fall of 1938, it became necessary to find a way for the Sternbergs to emigrate as quickly as possible, and Donata Helmrich methodically went to work. She went to the English Consulate, avoiding the long lines of people out front all waiting desperately for a visa by telling the guard she didn't want a visa, only information; and with that she was inside. First of all, she inquired about what documents were needed and what preconditions had to be met to obtain an entry visa for the children. There was no time to be lost, and so she wanted to make sure her protégées would not end up in the bureaucratic maze and all her efforts would come to nothing. Once she had the information, she went to England. With the help of some good friends there she enrolled the Sternberg children in British boarding schools, not an easy thing, for the tuition was very expensive. And so Donata was happy and grateful when she was able to find generous donors who would pay the expenses for all four children. But even now some difficulties remained, for she had to assure the authorities that the children would be taken care of and paid for during the long vacations, when the schools were closed. Otherwise, the whole enterprise would come to nothing. Luckily she was able to solve that problem too. Captain Foley, the Brtish Passport Control Officer in Berlin, made out the visas for the "Ingemannen" and their brothers. This man's name had apparently been secretly passed on from person to person. The full extent of all his good deeds in saving lives became known only much later. Frank Foley worked for the British Secret Service, his job as passport officer at the consulate was only a cover. He used his position to make out visas for many persecuted Jews. That was in clear opposition to the regulations of the British Interior Ministry as well as the Foreign Ministry. For they wanted to keep the number of immigrants low, much like all the other countries.

In February 1939, the Sternberg children set off for England, where they stayed for about a year. Their parents managed to emigrate at the very last minute, just before War broke out. Later the whole family went to settle in Brazil.

After that we lost track of the Sternbergs. We never heard from them again.

11

September 1, 1939, the day the German Wehrmacht invaded Poland, thus starting World War Two, marked more than the end of the Helmrich family's summer vacation. Sooner than planned, we left our summer quarters in Keitum on Sylt and returned to Berlin. Grandmother Zazi soon afterward said goodbye to us and moved to France where her son, my Uncle Prosper, had been working for a German company. He had decided not to return to Germany. He joined the Foreign Legion and eventually became a French citizen. Our grandmother, whom we loved, but sometimes also feared, had always played an important role in the family. Now she had left us. First she went to Nice; later when the Germans occupied France, she moved to Zurich. It would be ten years before she came back to Germany, and then it was only for a visit.

Now abruptly the situation for the German people changed. Ration cards for food and clothing were distributed, and private cars soon disappeared from the streets and highways since gasoline was available only to those with a special permit. An order was issued to black out all windows after sunset to protect against enemy planes. Women were recruited to work in armament factories; Jews and "foreign racial groups" were put into camps and forced to do slave labor. "Foreign workers" from the occupied territories were recruited as workers and laborers. Listening to foreign radio stations was forbidden.

With the start of the war, Jewish prospects for escaping from the Nazi terror suddenly diminished. Only a very small number were still able to leave the country. From October 23, 1941 on, emigration was prohibited.

Berlin had the largest Jewish community in Germany. In

1933 a little more than 160,000 Jews lived the German capital, constituting 3.78 percent of the city's total population. (Most of them were German citizens. By comparison, today there are about 400,000 people living in Berlin who are not German citizens but citizens of other countries.) By September 1939, 80,000 of them had emigrated abroad. The other half, those Jews who remained behind, had no means of earning a living, their savings were in frozen accounts, and they had no access to these or their other assets; they were wholly subject to the regulations of the labor administration; and any contact with the "Aryan" population was more than ever tabooed. In the same month the war broke out, the Nazi leadership were already discussing plans for deporting German Jews to Polish ghettos.

In December of the prior year, the last of the original six thousand Jewish specialty shops were closed or the owners were forced to sell them to an Aryan for a pittance. And in November, so as to close any loopholes that might allow Jews to earn any money at all, it was ordered that from January 1, 1939 on, Jews were not allowed to offer goods or commercial services for sale at any kind of market, fair, or exhibition."

For years there had been a stall selling sweets at our market on Preussen Allee in Neuwestend. It was run by two elderly Jewish sisters whom we knew only as the "little old women." Every Tuesday and Friday my mother bought things at their stall. Then, overnight this way of earning a living was denied them. But they didn't give up – somehow they managed to get the ingredients for preparing their sweets, and so during the next two and a half years they went door to door peddling homemade candies and chocolates, trying to sell their wares to their old customers. Apparently they were able to keep their heads above water, if only barely. They lived with their brother, a tailor. Now the Helmriches had him make or alter clothes for them. "As long as he's still here, we have to support him, no matter whether the things fit well or not," my father said.

As long as they were still here? Even before the infamous Wannsee Conference about the annihilation of European Jews, the so-called resettlement of Jews wasn't just a rumor. The transports to Eastern Europe had already begun to roll.

In the wartime fall of 1941 the "little old women" rang one last time at the Helmrich front door to offer their sweets. At that time they asked my mother to do them a favor. They took a small scale, some cellophane bags, and rubber bands out of a bag they were carrying – all precious items for that time. They asked whether they could temporarily leave the things there and have my mother put them away until they came back. They explained that they and their brother had received a letter from the authorities in which they were informed that they would have to leave Berlin on a transport.

The three were probably among the 4,200 Jewish Berliners on one of the first deportation train transports headed East to Lodz that left from Grunewald Station from October 1941 onward.

Sometime later I asked my mother, "Couldn't you have saved them somehow?"

"No, that wasn't possible – you simply couldn't save everyone." Her despair at being so helpless and also at her young daughter's lack of understanding were obvious. It may sound crazy or sentimental or superstitious, but she did keep the "little old women's" treasures – she simply couldn't bear to throw them away. And today the little scale, the cellophane bags, and the old rubber bands are in a box in my older sister's attic.

First day of school, Berlin, 1941, Cornelia second from left

12

I started school in September 1941. In addition to the photo above there is also another one which, unfortunately, I can't find – the inevitable first-day-of-school picture showing two thin little girls with gaps in their teeth and the cardboard cones filled with sweets that German children get when they start school. The little girls are my best friend Margrit and me. We're are standing in front of the massive school building on Leistikow Strasse.

It's an exciting day for any child – something new is beginning. Lots of adults tell you with knowing expressions that this is the start of the serious side of life. At any rate when I was a child, people said such things. For me, Cornelia, at the age of six, the words about the seriousness of life had a much deeper and far-reaching significance than most of those saying the words could have imagined.

My mother thought that this was the time to take me into her

Cornelia, summer 1936, Sylt   Cornelia, 1937, Berlin

confidence, to induct me, so to say, into the political family secret. I was to be prepared before I was exposed to new influences in school, just as my older siblings had been. I was now leaving the safe precincts of home, family friends, and the children with whom I was allowed to play. And therefore, my parents thought, I needed different protective mechanisms. I shall never forget that moment.

My mother asked me to go for a walk to a nearby park, which was quite unusual. She had little time for me and she hardly ever did this, and anyway I didn't think she really felt much like taking walks in those days. I sensed that there must be some special reason for this and was eager to find out what it was. Where do you start when you want to explain something very important to a child, something the child can't properly understand yet? It was disappointing to have my mother begin with some general comments about school, the teachers, and the other children. I was wondering why she was talking about such boring things. But then came her real message: I would hear things at school with which she and my father totally disagreed. And I must not believe a word of it! But I must under no circumstances talk about it. I had to keep mum. To impress me with the seriousness of our situation in a way a child could understand, she invented a new Grimm fairy tale, or at least she changed an old one in a very unusual way. It was the fairy tale about "The King of the Golden Mountain." He had been very evil, she said, and would not put up with any contradictions. But if someone did dare to cross him, then he would become furious and shout: "Heads off, everybody's except mine!" and whatever he commanded they did. "That's the kind of man who is ruling our country, and his name is Adolf Hitler." And mother explained that if Hitler found out about any of the things we talked about at home he would not like it. And that she and my father would like to keep their heads on their shoulders. I had to understand – I was old enough now – that I must not say anything at all, just like my sisters and brother. They had known about this for a long time already. "You can say anything at home, just as we do. But not to anyone else!" I gave her my solemn promise.

What does a six-year-old feel like right after having been entrusted with such an important secret? I probably understood back then that what my mother had just told me was serious and important, but I couldn't possibly have understood the full drama of the situation. But I still remember that I was incredibly proud that I had suddenly been, as it were, raised to the level of an adult. It was exciting, and I felt superior to all the other children. In my imagination, of course, my parents were the good Kings, the shining knights who dared to defy all evil and in the end would stand before all eyes, richly rewarded and heaped with honors.... That's what happened in fairy tales.

Now I was curious about what I was going to hear at school and what it was that my parents found so objectionable. Because I couldn't quite imagine it.

At first our lessons in school were no different from those

of other first graders in other times – except that we didn't say "Good morning" when our teachers entered the classroom, but "Heil Hitler." After a while, though, I noticed some other things – we learned songs I hadn't known before. And I knew a lot of songs, because I loved singing. We had to march in neat columns around our gym, and sing "*Wir sind des Führers jüngste Schar, Heil! Adolf Hitler, dir....*" (We are the Führer's youngest troops, Hail, Adolf Hitler...) I still remember a satirical song that I liked because it had a lively melody. The text meant nothing to me, but I still remember all the lines:

> "*Töff, töff, töff – wer kommt da angefahren?*
> *Töff, töff, töff, in seinem Kinderwagen?*
> *Töff, töff, töff – wo will der Jude hin?*
> *Er will wohl nach Jerusalem, wo alle Juden sind.*"
> Toot, toot, toot – who's coming down the road?
> Toot, toot, toot – in his baby carriage?
> Toot, toot, toot – where does the Jew want to go?
> He probably wants to go to Jerusalem,
> where all the other Jews are."

I sang this little song with the other children on the way home from school, joyfully at the top of my voice, repeating it over and over in a kind of endless loop because it was fun. When I sang it for my mother at home, all hell broke loose. She explained to me that she didn't like the song at all, not one little bit. That was probably why I remember it so well.

As the months passed, between arithmetic, writing and reading – in "German script" which practically no one can read anymore today – we kept hearing about Adolf Hitler and the brave men of the SA. We heard of a dead young man named Horst Wessel, and we learned "his" song, the Horst Wessel Song. "*Die Fahne Hoch, die Reihen fest geschlossen...*" (Raise the flag, in closed ranks…). The song became a second national anthem, and one heard it everywhere. Our white-haired teacher, Miss Seek, was probably one of those innumerable sentimental women who were crazy about Hitler. She was a "confirmed Nazi," my father told my girlfriend Margrit, with whom he liked to argue. Yet she didn't denounce anyone, even though she had the chance to do it.

All this made no impression me. I just felt superior and thought, "See, I know everything better than you." And I remained resolutely silent.

There was something else, though, that was more difficult. More and more often there was talk about the war and the "front," words that didn't mean anything precise to me. Every now and then they would say someone had "fallen," and I knew this meant he was dead and wouldn't come home again. It made me afraid. Most of my classmates' fathers had been drafted into the army. My father had been too, but he was too old to be sent to the front. And my brother was still too young – he was seventeen and in high school.

I had mixed feelings: Hitler was the evil King and the war was his fault – but the foreigners shot and killed the fathers of my classmates. I remember, there was one single moment when I was in danger of breaking my unshakable silence. Marion, a girl in my class, lived only a couple of houses down the block from us, on Westend Allee, and we would walk home together. One day she told me that her father was now "in the war," and I sensed how sad it made her. When we were almost home, I thought I would ask if her parents liked Hitler, and tell her that mine couldn't stand him. But at the last instant something kept me from doing it, from breaking my promise. I decided I would ask my mother first. Luckily she didn't scold me but just made it clear to me that the same thing went for Marion as for all the others. Hadn't I noticed that she had never invited Marion to come to our house to play with me? So there. Her family were most likely Nazis. And that was that. My playmates were hand picked for me, something that was much more common back then than it is now. But social background had less to do with it than the political views of the parents. You had to be sure with whom you associated; and that applied to the children too.

13

Even before I started school there had been other changes in our family. A week after she graduated in March 1941, my oldest sister was drafted for one year into the "Reich Labor Service." That was of course compulsory and one couldn't get out of it. The young women were called "*Arbeitsmaiden*" (work maidens) and were ordered to help out in agriculture or other tasks. They lived in camps and worked hard; in their free time, the leaders now and then would invite young soldiers or SS men. These "boy-meets-girl" events were part of the program. The togetherness was promoted, and sometimes it seemed as if these meetings were also supposed to serve the continuance of the Germanic race.

Now my much-loved sister was gone, and with her the piano music, which I missed very much, especially in the evenings as I was going to sleep. Our house had become quieter. Even though there were people coming and going every day. But the music had stopped.

A second change affected my father – early in the summer of 1941 he was inducted into the Wehrmacht (the army). Suddenly one day he stood before me in our dining room wearing a gray uniform. He looked good in this new get-up. "Is my father a soldier now?" I asked him. He smiled gently and simply said, "Yes." His answer sounded subdued and not at all enthusiastic. Would he have to leave now? Would he be able to come home on Sundays? No, that wouldn't be possible in the foreseeable future. He had to go far away, to Poland. But there'd come a time when he could come back to Berlin on a furlough. Furlough, that was the word the grown-ups used for "vacation."

My feelings alternated between pride in my handsome

soldier-father and fear of a long separation from him. When my mother appeared in the doorway and I saw her face, all my pride melted away. There wasn't the least trace of a smile on her face, not even a tiny mocking spark in her eyes – she was quite simply desperately unhappy.

For me, the departure of my father signified an end to our excursions to the country, no more "piggy-back rides" six feet up, no strong shoulder to cry on, no more encouragement when I felt I'd been treated unfairly, no affectionate pats on the head. When I saw him again, months (?), a year (?) later, his blond hair had turned snow white.

Eberhard Helmrich was sent as a Wehrmacht officer to the Province of Drohobycz in occupied Poland and given agricultural assignments. He moved into a house on Sienkiewicz Street assigned to him. The house had belonged to the architect Dörfler. The rightful owners had had to pack up their things and leave the house within twenty-four hours. Later, after the war was over, my father told us that in the early days when the Wehrmacht was in charge of the administration of the area, there were no persecutions, with one exception, Borislav. That would change radically with the arrival of the Gestapo and the SS. This marked the beginning of a time of terror and complete lawlessness and injustice. Arrests, mass shootings, and *Aktionen* (operations) were everyday occurrences until, with the implementation of the "final solution," the mass deportations to the extermination camps sealed the fate of the Galician Jews.

Helmrich didn't stay long in the Wehrmacht. He became a civilian employee of the *Generalgouvernement*, and in the position of District Farmer he was in charge of the department for food and agriculture. His superiors, who were headquartered in the Galician capital Lemberg (now Lviv), 37 miles (60 km) away, frequently urged him to become a member of the NSDAP, the Nazi Party, but he refused. The reasons he gave them for his refusal were that he had "religious scruples," and that the gentlemen had to make up their minds whether they wanted to have a farming expert or a Party member. This deviated somewhat from the usual pattern. Surprisingly his answer worked – they soon left him alone. Their only comment was, "The main thing is that everything goes well in the District." By that they meant the supply of food, which was very important to the German occupation forces. For the native Polish, Ukranian, and Jewish population supplies were at least to be regulated.

Drohobycz is a small city in eastern Galicia located in the northern foothills of the Carpathians. Today it is part of the Ukraine. It was founded in the eleventh century, and from the fourteenth century on, it was a center for salt production. The old city coat of arms showing nine salt barrels can still be seen today over an archway. In the nineteenth century oil was discovered in neighboring Borislav, and there was a regular "boom." From that point on many residents in the petroleum producing district lived from trade and the petroleum processing industry, even though the surrounding region continued to consist primarily of agricultural estates and farms.

Early in the last century the city of Drohobycz had 35,000 inhabitants, forty per cent were Jews, thirty-five percent were Christian Poles, and the remaining twenty-five percent were citizens of various other European countries. As a result of the Hitler-Stalin Pact, this part of Poland went to the Soviet Union and was occupied by the Red Army and thoroughly exploited and maltreated. With the German invasion of the Soviet Union in 1941, at least 539,000 East Galician Jews fell into the hands of the SS and their death squads. At that time this region had the densest Jewish population in all of Europe. And how many of these Jews were left after the Germans withdrew? Reports in the number of those who survived to be liberated by the invading Soviets three years later in the summer of 1944 vary. Historians estimate that there were about five thousand Jews, less than one percent of the original population. In Drohobycz and Borislav only a few hundred survived.

Even before Eberhard Helmrich arrived in Poland, he was indignant and angry about the fate of the innocent people who had had been deprived of their civil rights and property, and his opposition to the regime grew with each new display of inhumanity and arbitrary violence. But he had no idea what he would find in Poland. There everything was infinitely worse.

What was he going to do to be able to continue to "face himself in the mirror"? When he decided to help people wherever and as much as he could, he knew that chances were 95:5 against him. Later he talked about how desperately lonely he was – his wife, his family, his friends were all far away. And so he arrived at his dangerous decision all on his own, there was no one with whom he could have discussed it. The clarity with which he drew the sharp line separating himself from the majority of his "national comrades" gave him the patience, the calmness and confidence that were a prerequisite for succeeding in these efforts. "Only by having this confident certainty," my father wrote me much later in a letter, "was I able to cheat my way through." For the smallest sign of fear or uncertainty would have put an end to my life."

The "Jewish Policy" took its relentless course – all Jewish inhabitants had to be registered and they were obligated to wear the yellow star. This was followed by forced resettlement into crowded Ghettos and the confiscation of all valuables. In early January 1942, Galician Jews had to turn in their furs and skis for the German Eastern Army. To make sure these things were turned in, the Gestapo took hostages from among the members of the Jewish Council. These "Jewish Councils" were a truly fiendish arrangement. Their official assignments included supplying workers and establishing a system to keep order. But in reality they were used to put pressure on the Jewish people ostensibly entrusted to them. In other words: They were supposed to do some of the Gestapo's dirty work for them. The Germans often enticed them to do this with promises that were never kept.

District farmer Helmrich contacted the local Jewish Council to sound them out about how best he could help. There ensued a close but extremely dangerous collaboration. The Gestapo, Sipo (security police), and SS were all part of the danger – but how could one be sure that someone in the Jewish Council would not, in the hope of being rewarded, act as an informer? Such things had happened.

As his regular contact Helmrich chose a leading member of the Drohobycz Jewish Council who had once been a lawyer. Dr. Maurycy Ruhrberg. In addition to being in a constant state of terror, the people living there were plagued by hunger and starvation. In 1941, part of the harvest had been destroyed by flooding; this catastrophe and the cold winter of 1941-42 – commonly called the "*Gefrierfleischwinter*" (Frozen Flesh Winter) caused many deaths. The Jews suffered the most. Many collapsed on the street and died of exhaustion.

Together with Dr. Ruhrberg, Helmrich found a way of distributing food from army stocks to the hungry, especially to the children. A leading doctor at the Jewish hospital, Dr. Leon Miszel, came to Helmrich and told him about the dire situation of his patients. He and his colleagues were trying desperately to treat them, but most were dying of malnutrition. From that day on, the Jewish hospital received food and milk deliveries. Of course, supplying them with the means to stay alive was not what those in power desired, in fact, doing so was strictly forbidden. Therefore, it had to be done in utter secrecy. All this didn't keep members of the SS and the Gestapo from going to Jewish doctors for treatment when they got sick, as private patients, so to speak.

By the spring of 1942, a plan had been worked out that, at first glance, seemed quite innocuous, but which turned out to be an effective means of saving people. After many discussions with Ruhrberg and the Jewish engineer, Naftali Backenroth, Helmrich decided to set up a vegetable and fruit farm where as many as two-hundred-and-fifty young people could live and work, and, it was hoped, would be protected from the Ghetto and the constant persecution threatening them. The local authorities gave permission for the undertaking – the prospect of fresh fruit and vegetables for members of the Gestapo, the Sipo, and other privileged people was so enticing that Helmrich succeeded in getting the Gestapo to give him sole responsibility for the project. They agreed that no one would try to interfere with his management.

Helmrich and his cohorts chose Hyrawka, a small, deserted, and neglected farm about a mile from Drohobycz. There were old ruins and stables for animals. In a short while they added a carpentry shop and new greenhouses. All of it a bit jumbled, unmethodical; it would provide good hiding places.

Back then, Leopold Lustig (who would later become a dentist and Harvard professor) was seventeen when his father took him from the Ghetto and brought him to the farm. He remembers, "Helmrich had set up the vegetable and fruit farm so that the Gestapo could have fresh vegetables – and to save our lives. We went up and down the rows, digging up the beds; we pulled weeds, even before any were growing; we dragged bricks from one place to another. Each cucumber and each tomato went to a central place, so that no one would find out that there were more workers than tomatoes." To be precise, Hyrawka was a bogus company, a forced labor camp that wasn't really needed.

14

The greatest value of the farm was the relative safety it provided for the young people who could live and work there. They not only pulled weeds, they told jokes, they were joyful, and they flirted with each other – after all these were seventeen- and eighteen-year-old boys and girls. They were moderately carefree.

Yet the murderous lot really couldn't leave the farm completely alone as they had promised Helmrich; they simply couldn't bring themselves to do that. During the larger Gestapo roundups, Ukrainian militia and municipal police units – both infamous for their brutality – repeatedly tried to get into the farm camp and arrest a couple of people. Alfred Schreyer, who will be mentioned again later, remembers an incident that happened in the carpentry shop where he was working. He was twenty years old at the time. Two Ukrainians came in, looked around, and grabbed an old man who was sawing up some wood. "You're coming with us!" they yelled at him, pulling him by his long beard. "You're too old to work."

One of the young people working there had sneaked out as soon as the Ukrainians arrived and gone to look for "the Major" as they called Helmrich. Luckily he was nearby, came over, and barked at the two militiamen – what was the idea of just turning up here and annoying his people.

"We're taking this old Jew," they answered gruffly, grabbing their victim by the arm to drag him away.

"Nobody's being taken away here," the "Major" thundered at them as he grabbed the man's other arm.

Years later, Schreyer told me about the tragicomic scuffle that broke out. "With the old man in the middle, the Ukrainians tugged on one side of him and your father on the other." After a few seconds the two Ukrainians gave up and left in a rage. For the moment things had gone well. "He was like a shining light in that dark time," Schreyer said of my father. "He protected us; he was kind. When he was there, we felt calm. He was like an angel." That's what he must have seemed to them.

When there were "operations" by the Gestapo or others, Helmrich usually stayed at the farm camp day and night, and was thus able to prevent any arrests. Whenever raids were expected, he would hear the rumors beforehand, and Hyrawka would serve as a hiding place for the relatives of the girls and boys who worked there. They would leave the Ghetto and stay at the farm overnight or longer. With the help of Backenroth, the engineer, they had built a room that could be loosely sealed off with rocks so that it couldn't be discovered easily.

Many of the people he was protecting at this somewhat unusual forced labor camp, gained time there, a priceless gift – time to prepare an escape, time to eat enough to regain their strength, or to conserve their strength. Dr. Miszel, who survived in the secret room, later said he was convinced that it was because of the relatively good physical condition the farm-camp people were in, that most of them could withstand the terrible deprivation to which they were later subjected.

In May 1943 came the order to "get rid of all Jews immediately." There were few life-saving legal hiding places left in any of the factories or businesses essential to the war effort. But Helmrich managed to get some of his people jobs with the Raffinerie-Süd (Refinery South) and in an automotive workshop of Carpathian Oil. However, he couldn't prevent the closing of his fruit and vegetable farm. By the end of the summer in 1943 it was gone.

One means used in many rescue scenarios was to say that the Jews were specialists, even if they actually had no inkling of the specialty they were so urgently needed for. You went to the SS or the Gestapo and "requested" these people, and some of them were even taken off the deportation trains. The "you" here refers to rescuers like Oskar Schindler, Berthold Beitz, Eberhard Helmrich and a few others who were similarly engaged in saving Jews.

It was a bitter battle for time they fought – each month, each week, yes, even each day gained could make the difference between life and death. These were desperate attempts. And in the end most were in vain.

The most important thing – and it was more difficult than anything else – was to help persecuted Jews escape. "Papers" could be bought on the black market, and Helmrich, as a working employee of the occupation forces, even had access to blank forms and stamps. In his office he had a person he could rely on. His courageous south-German secretary, Maria Jordan, helped and abetted him in his activities. Without her and without her mother who kept house for Helmrich, many of the things he accomplished would have been impossible. These brave women also belonged to the small group of people who sabotaged the "Final Solution." They, too, were risking their lives.

The "Major" was constantly hiding people in his house. People who were waiting until the time when they could escape. There were never fewer than two, and sometimes there were as many as fifteen at one time. It's not without irony that the big shots the District Farmer had to invite to his house from time to time were served their dinner by young Jewish girls, pretending to be Polish.

As I mentioned earlier, the most difficult stage was the escape. Any attempt to flee was rendered difficult because there was no country anywhere that would have taken in the refugees. So for the duration they had to hide from the reign of terror or to disappear to another city or even another country with the help of forged documents. The first problem they had to face was simply getting out of the city, in this case out of Drohobycz. The danger of being recognized was enormous, for everyone knew everyone else. No one was allowed to leave the place without a permit, and the Ukrainian police was posted at the train station and inspecting all documents.

But Eberhard Helmrich had thought of a way out. He and his daring Polish driver, Janek Wojnar, in separate official cars would each drive several refugees to villages in the area surrounding the city where no one would know them, and they could live under assumed names. Or they could take a train from the local train station to some distant destination. "We would drive right through the SS barricades, giving them a friendly wave," my father said years later. Smuggling human beings right past the eyes of the murderers!

With the help of brave Janek Wojnar he managed to get the four-member Kilian family, former landowners, to Hungary. He helped a Mrs. Grauert and her two children get to Italy. In the same way and with the use of false names he managed to get out a Dr. Crailsberg, the Chairman of the Jewish Council Rosenblatt's daughter; his dedicated comrade-in-arms and confidant, Dr. Ruhrberg's wife, and at least twenty other people out of Drohobycz and to safety in Western Poland where no one knew them.

Helmrich was constantly trying to think up new ways of saving people. When he told Dr. Ruhrberg about a daring plan he had devised, the latter was at first quite alarmed. The plan was to send young Jewish girls and women who were furnished with false papers identifying them as "Aryan" Poles or Ukrainians, to Berlin. There, his wife would meet them and get them jobs as household help with German families. A rescue in the eye of the hurricane? Ruhrberg had his reservations about this. But Helmrich was sure that, because of the labor shortage in Germany and the large number of "foreign workers" there already, nobody would take the trouble of digging into the women's identities. And he thought the venture would work precisely because no one would be expecting anything so zany. He was right. In the months that followed, all the young women he smuggled to the West in this way survived the "Third Reich."

15

Visitors often stayed several days with us in our hospitable home in Berlin. Sometimes they stayed even longer. This wasn't unusual. But I do remember that I started wondering what was going on when we had a very quick changeover in housemaids in a relatively short time. They'd come, and then they'd be gone again.

Among them were two sisters, Susi and Hansi – back then they had different names. They were the daughters of Mr. Altmann, a friend and coworker of my father's in Drohobycz. Then there were Anita, Melanie, and Sylvia; there were also some young women who stayed with us who weren't Jewish, but whom my mother had taken under her wing for other reasons. I didn't find out till after the war what was really going on with all these girls, above all the Jewish ones.

Families who were having a hard time finding household help, turned to my mother because they had heard that her husband was posted with the *Generalgouvernement* as the District Farmer. They came to my mother to ask, "Could you get us a hard-working girl?"

They were of course overjoyed when their requests were filled. Overjoyed and completely unsuspecting. My mother would never have thought of revealing the truth about these young women, even to people she had known a long time. She would have endangered all the participants. And the girls, of course, would have been in danger of losing their lives.

Today, the stories of successful rescues leave one with a much-too-superficial picture. You can't simply shrug them off with "all's well ends well." A good outcome – and in this case what could really be called a good outcome? – doesn't give you any idea of all the obstacles that had to be overcome in the process, and also the lifelong trauma all those who went through it will suffer.

I'd like to retrace Susi Altmann's path to give the reader an idea of the great fear and incredible stress she had to deal with all along the way.

Susi and her sister had left Vienna with their parents in 1938 and settled in Drohobycz. They got to know Eberhard Helmrich shortly after his arrival there, in the summer of 1941. It wasn't long before they developed a close and trusting friendship. Helmrich appointed Mr. Altmann as his right hand man on the vegetable farm, and he, in turn, looked after the Altmann family. At that time Susi was still in Lemberg where, during the Russian occupation, she had been attending High School. Now she could neither leave nor stay, for since the Germans had marched in, a young Jewish girl was not allowed to travel, not even to join her parents. One day the bell rang at the front door of the family's house where Susi was staying. She went to open it, and the blood froze in her veins: Before her stood a tall German, and she feared for the worst. Instead, he politely introduced himself. "Miss Altmann," he said, "your father sent me. Quickly pack a few of your things. I'm going to take you to your parents in Drohobycz." ("He actually said 'Miss Altmann' and addressed me in a courteous way," she told us later.) For a few weeks Susi worked at the "Major's" house. But then, when it got too dangerous – Jewish servants in a German household were forbidden – she moved in with her family, her parents and sister, on the farm in Hyrawka.

Helmrich bought identity papers made out to "Helena Baran" from a Ukranian farmer. They had belonged to the farmer's dead daughter. Aryan papers were at a premium!

When my father came back to Berlin on furlough, my parents discussed the escape idea that had at first so shocked Dr. Ruhrberg. Donata agreed and lost no time in implementing the plan. She went to the employment office and applied for "a permit to hire a foreign worker for her household." She must have done this quite a few times subsequently too. My father returned to Poland and when he telegraphed his wife asking her to come to Drohobycz, it was obvious what it was for. She immediately set off for East Galicia to pick up Susi.

They shaved off the pretty young girl's beautiful thick eyebrows, braided her hair, and gave her high boots to wear. To complete the picture of a Ukrainian peasant girl, she put on an embroidered blouse and wrapped a colorful shawl around her shoulders. Almost nothing about her was genuine, except for her tears. And so she said good-bye to her parents and her sister Hansi, and trembling, climbed on the train to Berlin with my mother. They couldn't travel in the same car – and that was the next hurdle. The wife of a German occupier had to travel second class, while the foreign worker was forced to make the journey in "wooden class," that is, a third class car.

One of the first procedures she was subjected to once she arrived in Berlin was an examination in the Wilhemshagen transit camp, including a "racial" examination by so-called aptitude testers from the "Race- and Settlement Authority." The nineteen-year-old Suzi was terrified of that test, and refused to undergo it. She couldn't possibly go there, they'd immediately expose her. My mother did everything she could to reassure her and to make her understand that all of it was just a lot of pseudo-scientific humbug. "You've got to go there," she told Suzi. "If you don't, you'll really be in for it!"

The girl finally yielded to the inevitable, and my mother gave her a last bit of urgent advice, she absolutely must not use German numbers if she was asked to do any arithmetic. She explained to Susi that it was a natural reflex to fall back into one's mother tongue with numbers and calculations, and it was easy to fall into a trap that way.

Perhaps it was because it made my mother herself feel more

confident, or perhaps she just wanted to make it easier for Susi, but Donata accompanied the frightened girl and sat down in the waiting room. And she waited there for hours and hours, getting more and more uneasy. Finally, after seven hours, Susi-Helena appeared. She had gotten through all the tests including the skull measurements and was now recognized as a "very typical Ukrainian woman" and given permission to work.

But their sigh of relief was soon followed by the next shock. A Ukrainian, who looked after foreign workers from his country had found out where "Helena Baran" worked and, had come to look her up at our house on Westend Allee. He wanted to invite her to participate in the meetings of the Ukrainians working in Germany. She was afraid, but went to the meeting so that she wouldn't be exposed. She got the impression that they wanted to pump her for information and trap her into some careless remark. Each time she came back from one of these meetings she was more desperate. Occasional visits to our house by the police to check the papers of our "foreign workers" just added to her anxiety.

My mother felt great pity for her, but she was concerned that Susi would lose her nerve, that she wouldn't be able to withstand the constant pressure anymore. It might have turned into a dangerous situation, for the Helmrich family as well, and this had to be avoided at all cost. Especially because the Party and the authorities didn't have much trust in my mother when it came to her political views. Some Nazi official had once said in a threatening way that they knew how the wind was blowing in the Helmrich house, "but unfortunately we can't prove anything – not yet."

There was one way out of the dilemma: Donata had heard that a couple in Babelsberg were looking for someone to help with the housework, and so she was relieved to be able to send them the Ukrainian girl, Helena. The couple were grateful – and of course – completely unsuspecting. But here, too, the old game unfortunately had to be played: The Ukrainian *Betreuungsdienst* (Welfare Office) summoned them to a meeting, and the police also stepped in. Later Susi described, what she remembered as a particularly frightening walk to police headquarters. Mentally she had already said her good-byes to everyone as she started out – but it turned out there were only a few formalities to take care of. After that had been done she was permitted to return to her place of work.

And things went on like this, with increasing fear and anxiety and ever greater pressure, until the spring of 1945. Not until Germany's surrender and liberation did it stop.

In a letter to the Administration of Yad Vashem in the sixties, Susi wrote, "It's one thing to help someone escape from a country, but it's quite another matter to introduce a young person into one's own family. A family with four children…," and she continues, "How could Mrs. Helmrich be sure that I or one of the other girls she'd taken in, might not give herself away – in anger, or because we were caught unawares – and thereby endanger her employer and her children. When I think back to those days, I ask myself how she could live with all this worry for all those years until the end of the war…."

Hansi, using the name "Theodosia Pankiw," soon followed her older sister to Berlin. A trusted associate of my father's accompanied her. After a short time in my parents' home, she also found a position as a maid with a German family.

The two sisters didn't come back to our house on the Westend Allee often because it would have been too dangerous. But still, they thought of it as their home. "Donata Helmrich protected us as if we were her own children." Donata kept the two girls informed about life back in Drohobycz and passed on any news she gleaned from her husband's letters.

There was only one fact that she kept from the two girls until after the liberation. One day when "Major Helmrich" was away from Drohobycz on an official trip, the Gestapo had picked up the Altmann sisters' parents and killed them.

"When I found out that my mother was no longer alive, I started to call Donata Helmrich 'Mami,' and I pray that I will be able to keep doing that for some years to come." Susi wrote this in January 1986 to an acquaintance in the U.S. Three months later "Mami" was dead.

16

Although I knew that my parents were against Hitler and his regime, back then I knew nothing about their involvement in the escapes, and in hiding and smuggling people. My older brother and sisters of course had to be let in on what was going on. That was unavoidable. In retrospect I marvel at how smart that was on the part of my mother, for she apparently drew a line when it came to how much information a child should be burdened with. Perhaps it was also because the danger to us all from a thoughtless comment would have been too great.

In the meantime, the war had come closer to the civilian population too. For the first time they were subjected to nightly air raid alarms and had to follow instructions about going to air raid shelters when the sirens began to wail. Men who were appointed "air raid wardens" made sure that these regulations were obeyed. Our neighbors in the adjacent row house had had a small bunker built for them in their garden, and so it was arbitrarily decreed that my mother would go there with her children to take shelter whenever there was an air raid alarm. That was all she needed! Mr. Sch., the neighbor, was a member of the SS. It turned out to be an extremely difficult ordeal for my mother, as you can imagine. In the daytime I wasn't allowed to play with the neighbor's daughter Vera, but then at night we had to sit down there together and share our fear.

A plan was quickly made to dig a hole for our own bunker at the rear of our handkerchief-sized garden. Unfortunately, almost at the same time, some department – heaven knows which one – decreed that for official reasons and at official expense a large shelter was to be built for all the people living in the neighborhood.

Because ours was a corner property, people had access via a staircase to the garden. That, of course, was the very last thing the Helmriches needed. – I felt my mother's helpless anger. But there was no way of preventing it. Under German supervision, a construction crew made up of foreign workers from various areas moved in and started digging. Our entire garden and back yard would have been consumed by the project if something hadn't come up to stop it. I've forgotten just what it was, at any rate, it wasn't Mrs. Helmrich's anger.

Probably the authorities had, in the meantime, found a much more suitable, much larger site. And the way things happen in a bureaucracy, the hole in our garden was filled back up, and the construction crew vanished as suddenly as it had appeared. All that was left over from the digging operation was Josef, a fat, quiet, Belgian slave laborer who was to remain until the end of the war a most trustworthy and useful contact person for various of my mother's "deals."

We quickly had our own little bunker built. A contractor from the neighborhood, the father of one of my second sister's classmates built what was his idea of a secure shelter. Two large concrete pipe sections, the sort used in building sewers, were lowered into the ground. You couldn't stand up in the little room they formed, and of course there was no space for benches or chairs. The floor was covered with pillows on which we sat or lay. The seamless, round shape, our contractor explained, provided the best protection from the shock waves following an explosion. He was probably right. And so the family was by itself, although we sometimes shared the space with friends who happened to be visiting us when the air raid siren sounded. The grown-ups were certainly relieved to get away from the SS family and all the other strangers.

During air raid alarms the doors of all the houses and apartments had to remain open so that the rooms would be accessible and fires could quickly be extinguished. It was a very sensible measure. But it presented a problem for those people who were less interested in protection from the bombs than protection from being discovered.

We had air raid drills at school, and our teachers would take us children to a bunker. I wasn't accustomed to that, and I remember the first time it happened I really got scared. More and more frequently our lessons would be interspersed with stories of the war and "our brave Wehrmacht," and also what I assume was a lot of propaganda. Every day we sang "*Die Fahne hoch, die Reihen fest geschlossen…*" (Raise the flag high, our ranks are tight) or "*Wir sind des Führers jüngste Schar….*" (We're the Führer's youngest troops).

It must have been in the fall of 1942 that they introduced a new activity for schoolchildren. We were asked to bring in "old things." This included: paper, old clothes and rags, bones, and – by far the most valuable – old metal. The school principal came into our classroom one day to impress on us how important, more precisely, how important to the war effort our assignment was. The stuff the children collected was to be dropped off at the school. There it was weighted, and a list with the names of all the pupils in the class was drawn up on which the materials each child had dragged in and how much it weighed was entered. Once a week, I think it was, the teacher read out our names and the weight in pounds that each girl had brought in to be weighed.

For me this roll call, thought to be a valuable pedagogical incentive, turned increasingly into an hour of shame and humiliation. While the others were constantly trying to outdo each other in their collecting zeal – e.g., Ruth S.: 25 pounds newspapers – applause; Helga F.: 35 pounds old clothes – applause; Gerlinde L. – artful pause: 175 pounds old metal – frenetic ah's and oh's; I always felt a little smaller when it came to "Cornelia Helmrich's" turn, and a scornful "zero" would resound through the room, followed by hideous laughter. True enough, when

"Maud J." was called it was always followed by "zero" too. But that wasn't a problem because her father was a Swedish diplomat, and so it didn't really count.

At home I would beg my mother, implore her, to please give me something to take to school. But she remained adamant, explaining, "We don't give anything for Hitler!" When I finally came home one day crying uncontrollably and begged her to at least once give me something to take away my shame, she said, "All right, on Sunday we'll be having two little chickens to eat, and you can take the bones to school."

I felt greatly relieved carrying these remains from our Sunday dinner to school. Sad to say, the good feeling didn't last long. The next time Miss Seek came to my name and read aloud: "Cornelia Helmrich: 11 oz. chicken bones," the class broke out in uproarious laugher, the teacher frowned, and I felt worse than ever.

That wasn't the end of it though. My mother was summoned to the school principal's office. Maud's mother too. My mother, a gifted actress when it really mattered, merely acted clueless. She couldn't understand, she said, how they could burden such tender young girls with things like that, and at first, she said, she didn't want to believe it was really true. "Our children, being of the Aryan master race, are special, aren't they?" she asked innocently. (Just saying these words gave her a fiendish pleasure!) The indignant principal had to agree with her – how could she not. "Yes," my mother continued, "and that's why I simply can't understand why my clean little Aryan daughter should have to do this filthy work." The devil must have gotten into her, for she topped it with, "Rag collectors – that was always the lowest of jobs, wasn't it, and it was always done exclusively by Jews."

The principal must have been completely thrown by this one, for she didn't pursue the subject. Instead she simply dismissed my mother, saying that her daughter Cornelia would have to stay after school and write the sentence "I am supposed to collect old things" one hundred times.

My mother's answer probably didn't sound very friendly. "Of course Cornelia will do that if you think it's the right thing to do." Maud got away without any punishment. It was enough for Mrs. J. to stress her Swedish citizenship.

Meanwhile, I was waiting anxiously for my mother's return. As soon as she had told me that I would have to stay after school and I had expressed my dismay, she started to laugh. "Don't worry, child, I'm sure the principal will never mention it again, and you won't be staying after school or have to write that idiotic sentence." I had my doubts, but my mother was right. It happened just as she predicted – she'd obviously appraised the situation and the woman correctly.

The collection effort must have stopped soon after that. In any case, I don't remember this humiliating contest lasting much longer.

17

My girlfriend, Ursula Klein, was one grade ahead of me. She had to confront totally different hardships. She was an only child. Her father was a dentist and her mother a housewife – a good middle class German family. There was just one problem: Dr. Benno Klein was Jewish. The family had moved from Dresden to Berlin shortly after the Nazis took control of Germany because the Saxons were especially zealous and had banned Jewish doctors from access to the health care system in 1933 already. In Berlin they were a bit more generous. And so Ursula's father, a veteran who had fought on the frontlines in World War I, was allowed after some initial difficulties to get a license as a "Zahnbehandler" – a dental technician – as a Jew he could no longer call himself Doctor or use the title Dentist. He was permitted to open a health care system practice on Turm Strasse in the Tiergarten district.

Things went well until he had to close his practice in 1938. Now the family had no way of earning a living.

Luckily her mother found an office job in a bank. But then a new problem arose: What to do with their four-year-old daughter? There was no functioning nursery school, and in those days it wasn't customary for fathers to take over household duties or child care. So she was passed from hand to hand – a friendly family ready to take care of the little girl during the day, occasionally into a children's home. Sometimes things went well, sometimes not so well. The fact that Ursula was baptized as a Protestant made some things easier. For the father this circumstance turned out to be a blessing. Because of her Christian baptism he lived – in the Nazi terminology – not merely in a mixed marriage but even better, in a "privileged mixed marriage." Even so, this did not affect his being barred from practicing his profession. And like all other Jews, he was not permitted to travel, to leave the city where he lived. But as long as he didn't violate the laws, he was not subject to deportation. And in accordance with the meticulously thought-out hierarchy of deprivation of rights, privileged individuals like him didn't have to wear the "Jewish star" which Jews had been obligated to wear since September 1941.

In school Ursula, who was very bright, was considered by her teachers something of a class star. They consistently pointed to her as an example, often called on her, and encouraged her. Then, out of the blue, from one day to the next, it was all over. Her teacher – the same one I'd had problems with – started ignoring her model pupil. Ursula felt hurt; she could no longer understand what was going on in her world.

Her mother was indignant and went to see the teacher to find out what had happened and to tell her how much this sudden rejection had hurt her child.

"I really shouldn't be speaking with you at all!" the teacher said and explained what was behind it all. She had found out that little Ursula was "half-Jewish," and so she'd rather not have anything to do with her. Bad enough that she was allowed to be in her class!

And so Mrs. Klein took her daughter out of the school and looked for another solution. Not an easy task, for by this time the family was quite poor. Now they had to find money to pay for childcare. At first Ursula stayed with a family in Bavaria, in the vicinity of Munich. When that was no longer feasible because it got to be too much for the Bavarian family, she was put into a children's home in Bad Kohlgrub where she was constantly teased as "Jew child." This made her very unhappy. After that things got a little better for her because an affectionate woman in Mittenwald took her in, and she stayed there until the woman got sick and had to pass Ursula on to someone else. In addition to everything else,

Ursula was homesick and longed for her parents whom she hadn't seen for more than a year. This sort of unsettled life went on for little Ursula until the summer of 1944, when her mother decided to bring her daughter back to Berlin, which during those years was almost child-free. Most of the schools had been closed because of the air raids, and almost all Berlin children had left the city. They were either staying with relatives or friends in the country, or in the homes and camps of the Kinderlandverschickung (the Nazi evacuation of children to rural areas). During that time Ursula was tutored by a former teacher who was protected because he was in a "mixed marriage," but like her father, could not practice his profession.

After her return home, her parents explained to her that some of the family were "away." A cousin who was as old as Ursula and a "full Jew" had been deported with her parents to Lodz, and was later murdered. Her paternal grandmother had been taken from her apartment in 1943 and shipped in a freight car to Theresienstadt. But the elderly woman never arrived there; she died during the transport. "Your mother, the old Jewish sow, kicked the bucket," they told the "privileged" son when Ursula's father inquired about her. Ursula's grandmother, who had been a singer, had never lost her confidence in life. Hoping against all hope even as she was leaving, she called out to the woman who had been living with her, "And please hold on to my piano scores for me."

On her return home Ursula found herself in a changed Berlin – many of the people she had known were no longer there; the city was destroyed, the house they had lived in was a ruin; her family bombed out, like uncounted others. But finally she was back with her parents who were now living in the large, still-intact, apartment of her dead grandmother. They had squeezed together and were adding to the family income by renting some of the rooms. Until that apartment was bombed too. One of the people who shared their apartment, however, wasn't an "ordinary" renter, but really a secret guest. A woman in hiding. In 1943 Ursula's mother had taken Steffi, a Jewish girl, under her wing, and had fed and protected her until the liberation. Shortly before it was all over, in the winter of 1944/45, on top of everything else, it was discovered that Mrs. Klein had a serious case of tuberculosis. She couldn't risk going to a hospital because of what might happen to her family. And anyway, what would they do with her, a seriously ill woman who was related to Jews? So she postponed her hospital stay till after the war was over.

The family was in a public air raid shelter when the war ended. Steffi had escaped to a small garden colony and didn't come out of hiding till May 1945.

Once life began to return to normal, Ursula entered the Charlottenburg high school, where a special program was set up for children who, because of their "race," had not been getting a regular education. The family was able to move into a new apartment, where they were greeted by a grumpy janitor with: "And now we've got to live together with Jews!" Well, their former *Volksgenossen* or fellow nationals had to get used to that now, for better or worse. But most of them in Berlin and the surroundings were spared this, for there weren't many Jews left. In May 1945, there were only about six to eight thousand Jews in Berlin – four thousand of them had survived as partners in "mixed marriages"; barely two thousand survivors had returned from the camps, and some fourteen hundred (today it is thought that there were more) had survived to the end of the war and the Nazi terror, in hiding or with false documents.

18

In the fall of 1942 our mother took my oldest sister and me along on the extended journey to visit our father in Drohobycz. I still remember the overcrowded trains, the many soldiers, the gray- and clay-colored countryside, and the train stations teeming with people. The farther southeast we went, the more prevalent was the noisy clatter of wooden shoes on stone floors of the stations we stopped at on the way. We had to change trains at Przemysl, and there the clatter was so loud that you couldn't hear yourself talk.

In Berlin I'd seen people wearing seedy clothes from time to time, but here the shabbiness was everywhere. The crowds at the train stations seemed to be divided into two groups: Men in uniform and civilians in drab gray. I can't remember seeing anything colorful.

I could hardly wait to be with my father again. I was eager to see his house and how he lived, and long before we reached our destination I started that old guessing game, "How much longer till we get there?"

My father picked us up in his car at the Drohobycz station. Joyfully, I ran into his arms. He drove us to a spacious, yellow house, several stories high, on a quiet tree-lined street with front-yard gardens. I remember how disappointed I was because they put me to bed right after supper.

I no longer remember how long we stayed, whether for a few days or more than a week. I've also forgotten how I filled my days, and what the city looked like. But I do remember a very distinct difference between inside the house and outside. Inside it was bright, clean, and comfortable; outside, in the streets everything looked dirty and miserable. Here too you heard the clatter of wooden shoes everywhere. These are all fuzzy images, nothing more.

But three incidents made a deep impression on me and are unforgettable. We were in the car driving along a street when I noticed a frail, delicate girl somewhat taller than me dressed in rags. She is shuffling along next to a house wall; her head is bowed, her posture, peculiar. We must all have noticed her at the same moment, for as we drive past her, my father says very softly to my mother, "The poor girl, she's starving. By tomorrow she'll probably be dead." I'm sure I wasn't supposed to hear that.

I was horrified, and felt numb. I would have had so many questions to ask: Why is she starving? Why doesn't someone give her something to eat? Why don't we pick her up and take her with us? – But I didn't ask any of them. I pretended I hadn't seen or heard anything. I must have sensed that something monstrous going on here, and that you weren't allowed to get involved, to talk about it, not even with your own parents whom you trusted and who trusted you.

The second incident concerns a remark, nothing more than a scrap of conversation. My father had invited some people for the noonday meal, and I was allowed to join them. The table was beautifully set with a white tablecloth, and what impressed me especially, because I wasn't used to it, was that we were served by a maid. I don't remember any of the guests except for one woman. She was Polish but spoke German fluently. She was young, very pretty, and wore make-up. Her shiny brown hair was pinned up, and she was dressed in an elegant, gray, tailored suit. In the course of the conversation, of which I understood little, the beautiful lady said: "It's terrible to live in a country where babies are thrown out of the windows into trucks."

I remember nothing that was said before or afterward – only that one sentence.

I tried to make sense of it, tried to imagine the thing with the babies being thrown out of the window. I wondered whether I had misunderstood it. At the same time I knew that I had heard it correctly and that there was nothing to misunderstand about this sentence. I was silent, didn't say a word. Later too, after the meal, I still didn't ask any questions. There it was again, that limit set by one's self-imposed taboo.

The third incident was something completely different. It was exciting, wonderful, and filled me with happiness. My father took us on an excursion to one of the popular health spas in the Carpathians, Truskawiecz, famous for its fourteen different mineral springs. We drove through the sad streets of the city, then past an area with seemingly endless pipelines – they must have been part of the Carpathian Oil Company – after that the landscape became more and more beautiful, greener and more hilly. We made a brief stop. I still remember a typical circular flowerbed in a spa park with precisely measured plantings of flowers in ugly screaming colors. Happily we didn't turn back after that but drove on, farther and farther up into the mountains. That was adventurous enough, because in my entire life – all eight years of it – I had never been in the mountains. The green, green meadows and the tall pine trees – it was like an illustration in a picture book.

And then, once again, something was said that was probably not meant for my ears. "We're already in Partisan territory here – but it doesn't matter; they know my car," my father whispered to my mother. Still, I had heard it.

Partisans? I couldn't imagine what sort of people they might be. It sounded exciting and mysterious. Otherwise my father wouldn't have said it in a whisper. It seemed romantic to me, and at the same time I was reassured by his remark that they would recognize his car, and he didn't have to be afraid of them. But it seemed to me that other people definitely did have something to be afraid of – just not my wonderful, terrific, beloved father. And we didn't have to be afraid either because we belonged to him! I can still see myself sitting in the back of the car – blissful and glowing with pride because I was unexpectedly in on a secret, not unlike in school back home when I let the Nazi slogans bounce off me, with the uplifting sensation that I knew better than "they" did.

When we were back in Drohobycz, I saw no reason why I shouldn't ask. I wanted to know what was going on with these Partisans, who they were and why they knew my father's car. And so, my parents told me, that they fought against the Nazis and that was why they had to hide in the forests. The Nazis were searching for them and would kill them if they found them. At the same time I also learned that my father regularly supplied them with food. So that was why they knew him so well. Children love Robin Hood stories – and I was deeply impressed. I also knew, without being warned by my parents, that I had to keep my lips sealed and never speak about this experience and anything connected with it. And I never did. Of course I had no idea of the enormous danger my father was exposing himself to by doing all this.

The last memory I have of that trip is the red plush-upholstered sleeping car compartment on the train coming back to Berlin.

19

Four years later, in October 2000, I went back once more to Drohobycz. Through a series of amazing circumstances I had heard from a citizen of the town, who, as a young man, had known my father and often talked about him, especially when there were visitors from Germany. And he turned out to be the previously mentioned Alfred Schreyer. An elderly gentleman now with finely etched features, he augmented his meager pension by acting as a tourist guide. He showed tourists and interested journalists his city and told them a bit about the time before the war, but above all he spoke about the terrible years during the war when life was reduced to a matter of bare survival. And in most cases not even that was possible.

I asked him to accompany me. And so I walked through Drohobycz with the 78-year-old man, trying to remember, to think myself back into that time. Everything looked strange to me, but oddly enough, I recognized the house where my father had lived back then. It looked pretty neglected. The old yellow paint was flaking and dirty.

This little Galician city must have been quite lovely long ago and life in it peaceful. Drohobycz was not destroyed by bombs or artillery attacks. The conquest had been too quick, and the recapture of the city too. It was time that ruined it, bit by bit. At every turn we found decay, ruins, and deep poverty. The weekend market was well attended; the entire city seemed to be there, but the offerings were meager. It reminded me of the markets in Germany right after the war. And many of the market people, especially the old ones, reflected the desperateness of their situation in their faces. Many, Schreyer told me, don't know how

Alfred Schreyer, 2001 in Drohobycz

they could support themselves.

During my stay in the city there was running water only twice a day – three hours in the morning and three hours in the evening. Street lighting, where it even existed, was so scanty, that many districts were pitch dark in the evening and at night, and you had to grope your way with great care and skill over the ruined pavement. In the few available restaurants one sat in almost complete darkness at night; a light above your table was only turned on for you to read the menu.

The sad state of affairs in this once flourishing region was obvious. Whoever could, got by with barter and providing minor services. Poland across the border was a magnet in 2000 when I was there and so long as it wasn't a member of the EU, there were no visa restrictions for travel between the two countries. Young people took ramshackle buses; those who were better off drove across the border in their own cars. They bought things they couldn't get back home, smuggled them back into the Ukraine and sold them there at a profit. We also met a new group of "climbers," dubious "*bisinessmenni*" – they were young, preferred their outfits in black, mainly leather, and carried their mobile phones as visibly as possible. The young women confronted the misery all around them by wearing the shortest of miniskirts, the highest heels, and the most dazzling lipstick. Mr. Schreyer remarked about these nouveau riche, "They're making money dealing in dangerous business." He stopped and looked at me with sadness, "This has nothing to do anymore with culture as we understand it. It's all showing off. It's common ordinary showing off! Our culture is dead."

Alfred Schreyer was one of a handful of Galician Jews who were lucky enough to survive the Nazis. Each of the survivors has a story of his own. But their life stories have one thing in common: The first half of the 1940s determined their fate and marked them, psychologically and physically. None of them will ever be rid of the traces left by that time.

Schreyer guided me through the streets of the town where he was born and where his parents and grandparents had enjoyed a comfortable middle class Jewish lifestyle. His parents' house no longer exists; it was torn down and replaced by an ugly new building. The fine corner house where his uncle used to have a pharmacy has been occupied by a variety of tenants. We arrive at a street leading gently uphill. At its end stands an unusual, impressive building. As we get closer, I see that all that is left is the façade. Ahead of us lies, rather than stands, the totally destroyed ruin of what was once the city's large synagogue. Debris is scattered on the floor. Bushes and trees grow where once people prayed.

"After the war, those of us who were left, sometimes used it as a meeting place. But then it became structurally dangerous," my guide says. I ask him whether there are plans to reconstruct the Synagogue. He looks at me uncomprehending. "Reconstruct? For

Ruin of the Great Synagogue in Drohobycz, 2009
Wikimedia Commons, Birczanin

whom? There are no Jews living here anymore!"

There are moments when one is at a loss for words. In spite of the numbers that we all know by now; in spite of the reports, the personal stories; in spite of all the gruesome pictures of the Holocaust and the visits to former extermination camps – seeing this ruin whose reconstruction has become meaningless, made me suddenly see in all clarity the full extent of the obliteration of the Jewish population. I'm overwhelmed by this realization and cannot find the words to express my profound shock

This beautiful, ruined façade whose fate – to be totally demolished – is sealed, stands as the symbol of a centuries-old Jewish way of life, with all its vitality, piety, and cultural wealth. Destroyed, killed, exterminated – for a long, long time – probably forever. The land of Paul Celan, Joseph Roth, Manes Sperber, Rose Ausländer, and many, many other poets and writers is gone. Over, done with. Galicia without Jews has lost its special character. I am reminded of what Andrzej Szczypiorski said, namely, that the Poles without the Jewish Poles are a mutilated society.

I tried to imagine my father in this city during those years when killing and murder were everywhere. Doubtless, he, whom Alfred Schreyer had described as "our angel," had experienced occasions of inexpressible horror, had to witness what was going on without being able to do anything about it. How did he deal with the constant conflict between his official duties and his humanitarian commitment? He practically never talked about this. The truth is that he also was a small cog in the machinery of the murderous occupiers, just as all the other German helpers and rescuers in the East. They tried to interfere with the wheel of fate, and they succeeded in snatching a few hundred human lives from the grinding machinery – at the price of knowing what went on, being eye witnesses, and never being able to forget. And also the price of eventual failure. And thus, after the war, my father, and many others never found their way back, professionally into normal, everyday life.

We continued on our way through Drohobycz. Alfred Schreyer showed me another former synagogue. Today it serves as a warehouse. Here, one afternoon, two young SS men cold-bloodedly shot between seventy and eighty children who had taken shelter in the building after their parents were "picked up" never to be seen again. The German authorities had agreed to a request by the Jewish Council to find a solution for the children and had given permission for two women to be sent into the synagogue to provide the children with something to eat. Two days after this somewhat hopeful beginning, the two SS men suddenly appeared. "To find a solution?" they asked laughing, "We have a much better solution!" They leveled their weapons and fired and kept firing until nothing was moving anymore. They let the two horrified women live. Presumably on a whim.

A few steps farther on, Schreyer pointed to the place

where his teacher, the painter and the poet Bruno Schulz who wrote "*Zimtläden*," was shot crossing the street by the brutal SS Oberscharführer Karl Günther.

In 1942, Schreyer, then a young music student, became a slave laborer. He was put to work in a carpentry shop in Hyrawka and was thereby protected for the time being. He didn't really know anything about carpentry, but he wasn't the only one. He was skillful and strong, and worked hard, because he wanted to stay alive. After the Hyrawka camp was broken up, he had another stroke of luck. He was one of those who got a job with Carpathian Oil. In April 1944, only four months before the war ended in that part of Europe, there were cattle cars standing on the grounds of the plant, and all the Jews were put in the cars and taken away to an unknown destination. But in spite of everything, he and the others on the transport were somehow still hoping that they were being taken to another place to work. "I knew the country we were going through very well," the old man said. "And I knew that if the train were to continue straight ahead after a certain switching point, we'd still have a chance. But if it were to turn right, then we'd be heading for Krakow-Plaszow." The train turned right and headed for the infamous concentration camp. "We thought this was Hell – yet it turned out to be only a prelude to Hell." After a few months Schreyer was shipped to Camp Gross Rosen in Lower Silesia. There, after they had long ago taken everything from him, they now took away his last remembrance of his dead mother.

Schreyer's father had been deported to Belzec and killed there. His mother was shot in the nearby Bronitz Forest and buried in a mass grave. Twelve thousand Jews from the area around Drohobycz suffered this terrible fate. A forester who knew the Schreyer family, brought young Alfred a photograph he had found in the mother's coat pocket while he was following orders to sort the victims' clothing. It was a photo of Alfred, and in a moment when no one was watching, his mother had written on the back, "I am happy my son is alive. With his picture I go to meet my death." But then she wasn't allowed even this comfort because the victims had to take off all their clothes before they were shot. Alfred had been carrying this photo with him from the moment the forester gave it to him. In Krakow-Plaszow he was able to hide it on his person, but in Gross-Rosen in October 1944, he couldn't even do that.

His journey from one horror to the next continued: Schreyer was taken to Buchenwald and to the Aussenlager Taucha near Leipzig. After that he and the other concentration camp inmates were forced on insane, senseless marches like the ones we know from the written historical records. "On May 7, 1945, we saw the first Russian tanks, and ever since then I celebrate my birthday on May 8th – I have every reason to do so!" Schreyer told me on our walk.

He stayed in Germany until the fall of 1946, in the Soviet Occupation Zone, working as an interpreter for the Red Army. When the repatriation order came through, he applied for permission to emigrate to Buenos Aires where his uncle and aunt lived. They asked for their address, but that he didn't have. They left the decision up to him, but suggested he wait in a camp until his relatives could be found and all the emigration details were cleared up. Into another camp? "I was terrified. No, anything but that; I just couldn't. Not for anything in the world!" And so it happened that the twenty-four-year-old Alfred Schreyer at last, by way of several detours, returned to Drohobycz.

He barely supported himself by playing the violin and performing in a trio playing dance music. Then he went back to study, started a family, fathered a daughter and a son, and taught at the local Conservatory until his retirement.

In 1993 both his children emigrated to Germany with their families. They had lost all hope for an improvement in living conditions in the Ukraine in the foreseeable future. "This time being Jewish proved to be an advantage for us," Schreyer's daughter told me in a conversation we had. "Anyone who's young enough and has the chance to do so, will leave that country."

Only the old people stayed behind. At first the older Schreyers had wanted to follow their children. But then, once the documents lay on the table before them, they lost their nerve, and decided to stay in Drohobycz. "It is too late for us; we're too old," my companion summed up his story. "And besides, here I'm the Mr. Schreyer everybody knows – but who would I be in Frankfurt?"

Alfred Schreyer the musician wrote a song to commemorate the terrible fate of his mother and so many others. It is called "Bronitz Forest" and he has performed it often at Memorial events. The day before my departure he sang it for me in his beautiful strong voice. My voice shook as I thanked him.

20

When Alfred Schreyer says, "Eberhard Helmrich saved my life," it's somewhat confusing. It's really not quite true, but it isn't quite false either. He was protected because of his work until April 1944, longer than most, and he was armed against what was in store for him by being in good health and having had adequate nourishment – both prerequisites for surviving concentration camps and death marches. These didn't "make survival possible"; it would be cynical to say that. Perhaps we should say rather that they were preconditions for making survival more likely.

The stories of those who were saved and their rescue are not so clear-cut or simple that one could classify and label them. The rarest type of rescue was when one person was able to protect another from the very beginning right through to the liberation. Still, it happened. At the Center for Research into Anti-Semitism at the Berlin Technical University they start with a rough formula: At least seven people had to be ready to help in order for one life to be saved, and often it was more.

On the other hand, those same people at various times frequently also helped rescue other people. Not all helpers were active to the same extent or participated in the same way in a rescue – but just getting permission to hide for a few nights in a garden house could mean the difference between life and death. As I've said before: every day, every hour counted.

In Berlin alone two hundred cases of rescues that failed have been documented – one thing is certain, there were many, many more than these. Yet a rescuer who, while trying to rescue someone, fails in his mission, through no fault of his or her own, is nevertheless considered a rescuer. Many took their stories with them to the grave because both the victim and the would-be rescuer didn't survive or because they didn't feel like talking about it. Often the rescuers and the rescued were silent because they just wanted to forget, to erase from their memories that time with its dreadful images. Frequently they remained silent because they felt ashamed – some because they reproached themselves for not having done more, some because they survived while so many others were killed. We know of survivors who were afraid of the questions their children might ask, such as: "What did you do to keep them from taking you away?"

I met a man who, when his little daughter asked him what the number on his arm meant, said that it was a telephone number he never wanted to forget. A Jewish woman who survived as a child in Berlin, wanted to tell me the story of her rescue, but she kept postponing it. Finally one day she said with tears in her voice that she couldn't do it. Her memories of that time were too painful.

Those individuals who were honored later were identified by survivors only after many years had passed. They themselves never mentioned their deeds. "You don't advertise things like that," said a Berlin actress who had hidden a friend in her apartment.

In some cases there were helpers who asked that their names not be mentioned because they were afraid it might be detrimental to them if those around them found out. One of these was a woman from the former GDR, who asked that her mother's maiden name and not her real name be inscribed on the plaque and in the archives at the Israeli Memorial Site at Yad Vashem. It's hard to believe, but she was afraid of her neighbors. And this wasn't all that long ago!

This great act, saving a human life in a time of terror and subjugation, should be seen as one link in a chain composed of many links. Each of these links is of equal importance, for if only a single one breaks, then the whole chain breaks, and everything will have been in vain.

There were many nameless individuals of whom not even the victims knew that they had aided in their survival. The little old saleslady in the grocery store whom we'd baptized "Anna Littlehandful" because she always said, with a smile, that she had put an extra little handful of things into our bag of groceries – she must have had an inkling of what was going on. The rations allowed by our ration cards for those particular groceries were hardly enough for one's own needs; sharing them with someone else was quite a feat. There was the fish lady at our market who would wrap up more for my mother than she had asked and paid for, and who said with a poker face as she handed over the package, "Well, you always seem to have company, Mrs. Helmrich." Other market people behaved in a similar way when my mother turned to them because she needed "more today."

Police Officer Kellerhof, who indirectly but clearly warned my mother whenever inspections were to be expected. The mailman, Haibel, who not only delivered letters but also transmitted other information. Or Emmi Teschendorf, who owned a bakery and coffee shop, and would generously give us a piece of cake or even an entire cake for the ostracized ones, and in whose shop they could even secretly meet each other. No rescue would have been possible without the helpers, people who always had a bed available for overnight. Like mother's friend, Doctor Hildegard von Weber. "Hildegard you're getting a visitor today," my mother would announce, and then her friend would know what to do. Food ration coupons were given away – or what was even more desirable – cigarette coupons; clothes and blankets were donated and sick people in hiding were cared for – against all the regulations.

My parents' circle of friends consisted of such people – "a sworn community," as my mother later called it. Our neighbors, the Schlemms and the van Gülpens, belonged to it. They were called "the heroes of Westend Allee" by my sister, also because they were quick and very brave in extinguishing fires. If we had illegal "guests," our brave Hedda would stay with them in our house during nights when there were air raids. When the air raid warden reminded her that not going to the air raid shelter during air raid attacks was forbidden, she said that she suffered from terrible claustrophobia in the small shelter and couldn't stand being shut in there. Later she wrote about that to her one-time charge, Kurt Samolewitz or as he was now called, Moshe Zamir in Jerusalem. She wrote: "When there was an air raid alarm, the people we were hiding weren't allowed into the bunker, and the windows and doors in the house had to stay open. That way the Nazis could easily go in everywhere. I would stay in the house, so they couldn't just come in. I always told them everything was all right. Dear Kurt, I can't possibly write it all down; it was so awful."

After the war I once asked my mother, "By the way, did you know any Nazis?"

"Oh, yes – but only at a distance," was her answer.

Her first husband was also part of the network of helpers. He lived with his second wife and young son on Darss in Western Pomerania. Knowing full well what they were doing, he and his wife repeatedly took in Jewish women with false documents and employed them.

There was a big difference between a big city and the countryside. The anonymity of the metropolis made going into hiding much easier, whereas in a small town or village the social control was so strong that it was very difficult to escape scrutiny. A government decree dated February 5, 1940 says: "Jews must not be allowed to move from small towns to large cities. They are more difficult to keep under surveillance there." The countrywide deportations began in October 1941. In September 1942 the resettlement" of "full Jews" was considered "completed." The only place it took longer was in Berlin where it went on far into 1943. One reason for this was that, for one thing, prior to World War II, Berlin had had the largest Jewish community in Germany, and for another, because about half of all the attempts to go underground or escape deportation happened in Berlin and its environs. But here, too, either in the course of raids or through information provided by "alert" citizens, people who were fleeing or in hiding kept being discovered and sent to their deaths.

Two thirds of the rescuers in Germany at that time were women. Their husbands were fighting at the front. Most of the time the husbands knew what their wives were doing back home and had given their consent. Sometimes they were working as a team, like my parents. But unfortunately there were also those cases where the men did not agree at all with what their wives were doing, and in extreme situations they would even inform on their partners. One can only speculate what accounted for the remarkably high percentage of women rescuers. Was it simply the absence of the men? Or were women less easily intimidated? Or did this sort of activity engage their maternal instincts? Of necessity women's everyday routines were more organized, whether they were housewives, or had outside jobs – they regularly bought groceries, clothing, fuel, and other things. For that reason women were better suited to deliver food; they just looked less suspicious. And they also had more freedom in their activities than the men because these women hardly fit the traditional picture which saw them as dependent and obedient – not capable of taking an active part in civilian resistance! Whatever it was that turned these women into rescuers – they had courage, nerve, endurance, and a great deal of imagination and inventiveness. Danger and fear were ever-present. And knowing this, the documented accounts that tell about these women and their rescue efforts are that much more impressive. But what stood out during that period was the total lack of public confidence in the legal system. You never knew what might happen to you, especially since regulations were handled very differentially within Germany. This was a reflection of the different attitudes of individual Gauleiters (Nazi district leaders), mayors, and other authority figures and their power to implement these laws. Some very courageous people took advantage of this lack of confidence in the legal system. The danger to life and limb was incomparably greater in the occupied sectors in the East. There rescuers of Jews who were caught weren't even arrested first or put into a concentration camp – they were summarily put to death. In the Berlin dialect people called it *"Köpfchen kürzer"* (shorter by a head). I remember from my childhood this phrase being used quite often around me. Fighting fear with sarcasm. In an interview many years later my mother said, "You can't just sit and quake in your boots all the time – you simply can't. No human being can be afraid for twelve years, that's just not possible. You have to learn somehow to live with fear, and that *is* doable!" She knew the danger my father was in – and she had to "get used to" this fear too without putting any pressure on him.

21

In the East there was no network of helpers that even vaguely resembled the one in Germany – even though it was very small. There were scarcely any trusting friendships among the Germans; it was better not to trust each other.

But the number of people in the know, the group of people who were in on the secret was incomparably larger. Among the persecuted people, the victims, it was not possible to keep it a secret who the people were who were ready to help. So there must have been many hundreds who knew the names and addresses of their potential protectors. They were praised and even given "titles" – life-endangering titles. They called Berthold Beitz, a man who would later become a big industrialist, "Father of the Jews," and they called Eberhard Helmrich "King of the Jews." What fodder for the Gestapo! Both men were living in Drohobycz at the time. Beitz later moved with his wife and young daughter to the neighboring town, Borislav. District Farmer Helmrich helped the fourteen-year-younger petroleum manager Beitz in setting up a cooperative – "Zluka" – that maintained shops for his employees. It sold consumer goods to the workers; later there was also a bakery and even a pig-raising operation. The people were pleased with that, and the authorities could not raise any objections. These two Germans also saw each other socially, privately, but not too much; still, they did visit each other.

Thus it really is amazing that they never talked with each other about their humanitarian activities. They obviously respected each other, but they maintained their cover, preferring not to take any risks.

Berthold Beitz remembers a "thoughtful, very calm man who

probably wanted to protect us both by his silence. You can't reveal what you don't know. Not even under torture. His wife, Else Beitz, described Helmrich as "a very silent man," and she adds, "I had the impression that he lived in a world of his own."

I'm quite certain that even back then my father knew about Beitz's political views and his rescue efforts, for he mentioned it quite early on. I could have sworn to that. It's possible that others had told him about it, for instance, members of the Jewish Council. On the other hand, Beitz found out about his "colleagueship" with the older man only years after the end of the war. Beitz was never a member of the Nazi Party either.

My father must really have lived a rather withdrawn life during those years. He didn't participate in hunting trips, something he certainly liked to do in the old days. "(My siblings and I remember exciting late evening excursions to blinds, and I remember monstrous deer antlers hanging on the walls of father's room.)

It's not surprising that this world of mistrust, insecurity, and misanthropy provided fertile ground for informers. What is surprising is that there weren't more instances of betrayal. How could these men go on for years with their activities, how were they able to keep their heads out of the noose?

This is hard to grasp for readers today – but a Big Brother State, a land under close surveillance has its own prevailing logic. The people can't avoid the mixture of terror, fear, and faith in the infallibility of authority. And so the Drohobycz Gestapo was probably incapable of imagining that someone would independently and without protection dare to act as coolly as Helmrich did. My father, this image of an Aryan member of the Master Race – blond, tall, self-assured and high-minded – whom 'they' wouldn't have dared to touch. Arnon Gill, his very young Polish-German coworker in the office, had no doubt at all that this was the reason he stayed alive. The twenty-two year-old was of great help to my father. He spoke three languages fluently,

German, Polish, and Russian. But even more important was his absolute discretion. I met him many years later, shortly before his retirement. After the war he had studied at the university in Poland and taught in colleges, which eventually led him to the University of Freiburg. He told me how amused he was back then, watching my father carefully avoid saying "Heil Hitler" whenever it was called for. "He would approach official visitors and call out, 'Ah, we haven't seen each other for a long time!' or 'How nice that you came,' or something like that." Laughing, Gill told me that my father had hung the obligatory picture of Hitler on the wall above his desk. When visitors whom he knew well came to the office and sat down at his desk, he always asked them to excuse the fact that they had to look at the *Führer*. "I put him there so I wouldn't have to look at him," he would explain.

Of course Helmrich and his co-conspirators could never be sure, and there are reports from various persons which all agree in confirming that it was more than just a suspicion that Helmrich helped Jews and Poles – it was practically a certainty. The surprising conclusion was that the District Farmer must have had excellent connections with the "top people in Berlin" if he really brazenly did all the things they said he was doing, and that it would be best not to lay a hand on him. These gentlemen obviously didn't want to have a confrontation with "Berlin" and their higher-ups.

My father's civilian superior at that time, Hermann Görgens, made an enlightening statement in 1960. He was being interviewed about the District Government in Drohobycz at the time of the German occupation for the *Ostdokumentation* of the Koblenz Federal Archive. I cite here a very few extracts from the forty-page-long file.

The interviewee: "Mr. Helmrich was also in charge of feeding the Jewish population. I discovered quite soon that he apportioned more to them than was permitted. He was a man who was humanely open-minded, who appreciated beautiful things, almost an artistic person. He wasn't a farmer who stomped around in Wellington boots, talking about beef backs and pork backs, but a more theoretically minded farmer, a very fine human being. There was nothing to rebuke him for. And he was modest in the way he lived. I decided then not only to approve of his actions but also to consciously promote them and continue them."

"His household help didn't look typically Polish, the way a Polish woman would, but rather she looked more Jewish. I didn't say anything about it because I thought, if this was the case, it would be better not to talk about it. You never know how things will turn out."

"That was the Helmrich example. He went so far in individualizing his administration that he was clearly acting contrary to instructions."

This man, in his private life he was a lawyer, certainly wasn't a monster, but he wasn't a hero either. He would probably not be offended if one classified him as a well-educated pussyfooter – a common type.

Retrospectively, he glossed over the situation back then in Galicia, and according to his own statements, practically never saw or knew anything. When questioned about his own behavior back then, he said, "When members of the Jewish Council came to see me to discuss the distribution of some foodstuffs or to ask about passes, I would ask them to sit down and they sat down. But then the security police told me that it was not permitted to deal with Jews that way. So then, after that, I no longer asked them to sit down; instead, as soon as they appeared I also stood up. They couldn't very well order me to sit down during the session. But these were minor details in comparison to the rest of their tragic destiny; yet at the same time it was also an expression of the intention to alleviate and to help wherever one could. I hope that most Germans, if not almost all, essentially had a similar attitude." I wonder what his children thought of his statements. The reality was quite different. One day the inevitable happened: Helmrich was denounced by his colleagues who went with their complaint to the Gauleiter in Lemberg and the SS. It just happened that some high official of the SS Security Service was in Lemberg at the time, and he managed to extricate Helmrich from this great danger. "I know that you helped those people, but I'll see to it that you can remain in your position," he said to my father. Apparently he wanted my father to understand that he, his rescuer, knew all about him. But perhaps he was also a man with a certain degree of farsightedness – after all, who could predict how things would turn out eventually....

My father later said that even among the "SS there were men who had no blood on their hands." It is possible that extreme situations sharpen an individual's ability to read another's character; but it might also be that my father's cool calm in his dealings protected him.

In those times he was a man of interesting possibilities: He had control of food stores – including alcoholic beverages – as well as cattle and horses. According to many people who knew him back then and had contact with him, he never took anything in return for his help – no money, no gold, no diamonds, yet he himself bribed others without inhibition. He presented his "bill" in a different way. And he didn't hesitate in making use of members of the SS and the Security Police for his purposes. Thus, with their help he got people released from jail several times. Once even his faithful driver, Janek Wojnar, a Pole, whose nighttime rescue trips had come to light through a "tip."

But that didn't prevent him from getting rid of an unbribable official when he thought it was justified. I discovered a document at the Lemberg Central Ukrainian Archive signed by him and dated October 12, 1942. It is addressed to the Municipal Commissariat in Borislav. It read: "After examining it, I am returning the enclosed request. I do not see how setting up a buffet with a bar serving beer can have anything to do with Culture. Nor is it possible for me to make allocations for this project. The District Farmer."

22

Everyday life for the Helmrich family was on the whole not much different from that of most of the other families living in the German capital. Our mother tried to maintain a halfway normal life for herself and her family and to put edible food on the table. It is important to have an idea of the food situation of those years: There wasn't much of anything, and the good things, like real coffee, butter, or even southern fruit, were practically unavailable. Very rarely was there something sweet, and we children missed that very much. No chocolate! But then if, against all expectations, a little square of it turned up, it was hoarded and made to last for as long as possible. Now and then the exact opposite would happen: the market would suddenly be flooded, and for a few weeks some item, a particular vegetable would be available in great plenty, until you couldn't bear to see or eat any of it anymore. I have a disgusting memory of a flood of artichokes and a rhubarb infusion (sweetened!). My brother would come back from school at midday and ask with dripping sarcasm, "Well, what are we having today? Surely not…! Oh, artichokes, what a surprise!" It always was, and remained my mother's habit to serve food to her friends at our house or in her garden. The term "serve" is a bit euphemistic, for there was never very much food. But even the little we had was, whenever possible, eaten in the company of others. Magazines published helpful recipe hints, such as, "Make a lot out of a little" or "Delicious cake made from simple ingredients." None of it particularly convincing for someone who was as good a cook as our mother. She rarely tried out one of these frugal recipes, and the few times she did, the results didn't persuade any of us. I remember one dish, euphemistically called "*Holzknecht's Nockerln*" (Forester's Dumplings) the main ingredient for which was cornmeal, and was supposed to be something like Italian gnocchi or polenta. It didn't look bad when my mother brought it to the table. But it tasted awful and was hard as rock. The meal ended in general laughter; I think all of us felt full just from the intensive chewing. What was left over – unfortunately a whole lot of it – was later fried. That was a flop too. Another time my mother served a cake made from the leftovers of the *ersatz* coffee – popularly called, *Muckefuck* – and some other ingredient that was easily available. That experiment also ended with a rueful "never again!"

And so what she offered to us and shared with friends was whatever we had on hand or something someone had brought back from the country. And even if we only had tea with nothing else. As I remember it, we always had tea on hand. Where it came from and how, I don't know, but tea seemed very important. One of my mother's grim sayings was, "Hitler can force me to darken all the windows and prevent my getting sensible things to cook and bake with, but he can't keep me from having an open, hospitable house!"

My eldest sister did her one-year service in the country (*Landeinsatz*) as part of her compulsory labor service (*Arbeitsdienst*), and right afterwards she had to do other compulsory tasks. My younger sister left the Westend school and transferred to acting school. Our brother graduated and was drafted into the army. Our tireless Hedda took care of the youngest (me), and she made sure that there was some minimal degree of "order" maintained during these disorderly times. She considered it a personal insult whenever the sirens drove us to the air raid shelter before I had finished my supper.

The longer the war lasted, the more our days and nights were determined by the irregular rhythm of the air raid alarms and the all-clear signals. But the Helmriches were lucky because none of

114

the bombs struck our house. In fact, there was comparatively little destruction from the air raids in our neighborhood. Of course windows shattered everywhere because of the bomb blasts, but they were quickly covered again with cardboard or a sort of transparent synthetic material. Also, as was to be expected, fires broke out sporadically all around us. Whenever that happened the grown-ups went to put out the flames, for everyone helped everyone else. I recall that one morning when I was about to leave for school, I found my sixteen-year-old sister in my mother's bed looking pale and miserable. She had come home after a long stint putting out a nighttime fire suffering from smoke inhalation.

Besides these everyday occurrences there were the somewhat unusual things that kept happening in our family. My sister, while serving in the *Arbeitsdienst*, became friends with a girl, someone she could trust and with whom she could speak openly. This was a stroke of luck not to be underestimated. The camp where they were being housed was located between Brandenburg and Werder, in the outer zone of the anti-aircraft ring encircling Berlin. This meant that the anti- aircraft guns were very close by. One night, when the other girls were already asleep but the two friends were still talking, they saw a plane shot down not far from their camp. They looked at each other, and jumped up with the same thought in mind. Quickly they unlocked the barracks door, locking it again from the outside. Then they ran, with pounding hearts, toward the downed plane. They found the young English pilot, and seeing that he was only slightly wounded, they pulled him out of the wreckage. Then they turned on their heels and ran as fast as they could to the police station. They had only one thought at that moment, to prevent the SS from finding the Englishman and doing God-only-knew-what to him. The two nineteen-year-olds felt he'd be a lot better off if the police got to him before the SS did. It was all they could do for the young man. After that they returned to their barracks, relieved to find that no one had even noticed they had left. Today this might look merely like a youthful prank, but back then it could have had serious consequences for the two "work-camp girls."

My sister finally came home to Westend Allee a year later. Of course, after their labor service was done, girls couldn't do just anything they wanted to. Instead, having completed their compulsory service, they were assigned to a job. My sister was deployed to the Armaments Command for Berlin-Charlottenburg where she had to deal with the files of *UK-Gestellten* – draftees who had been excused from service for a time. The letters "UK" stood for "indispensable" – in this case it referred to men who were indispensable for duty at home, not for service at the front! My sister wondered about the fact that these indispensable men were practically all officers and that there were no common soldiers among them....

Even after a further year, the state still did not release her from service. The next step would have been a job as a helper in the war effort. However, there was a friendly boss in the armaments command who had a daughter of the same age. He "forgot" (what a coincidence!) to report her availability to the appropriate office. So in the spring of 1943 my sister was able to start her studies at the Music Conservatory.

At the same time our bother received his draft notice. He was in the middle of exams at Kant High School in Berlin-Spandau, an interesting school, even though he didn't like it, because the principal was an Anti-Nazi and because it was attended above all by students who had a reputation for not being politically "sound." There was no open discussion of this, but insiders knew about it. One of the students' "escapes" was listening to highly prized American shellac records. They listened in groups and swapped the records. Only people with extraordinarily good connections had access to them, for instance, someone who worked for the radio station and had access to the record archive... The kings of swing and jazz, Glenn Miller, Benny Goodman, Louis Armstrong, and Duke Ellington were their idols. They all went to the same dancing school on Lehniner Platz in Charlottenburg because there they could dance to the frowned-upon "Negro music." My brother still remembers that whenever Hitler Youth guys appeared on the scene to check on what was actually being played there, they immediately switched to records that were approved by the Nazis.

In the meantime his class had completed the written and the athletic exams for graduation; the other credits they got more or less for free, so that they'd at least have something to show when they came home from fighting in the war and wouldn't have to go back to school. Granted, many of them never came home.

My brother was first sent for military training to Poland; but soon after that he was posted to the front, to Russia. In taking the oath to the German swastika flag he secretly made the childhood *Blitzableiter* sign with his other hand (like crossing your fingers). He was assigned to the infantry, which was in urgent need of officers, and his superiors were quite surprised when he told them that he wasn't good officer material. When they asked why not, "after all you graduated from high school," he pretended that he was totally unable to give commands. ("Certainly not under this regime," he told us.) But he could carry out orders; that was no problem! His comrades and he never experienced any flush of victory, but they did certainly live through all the horrors of war. All they did was "march backwards," driven by the Red Army, of which they were all afraid. The Battle for Stalingrad was already over by then. Next he was assigned to setting up telegraph lines, and then he did an apprenticeship as a telegraph operator. He was awarded the Iron Cross Second Class like all those who had survived the exertions of the Russian winter, and still a simple soldier, ended up a Russian prisoner of war. He came home after three years of that, weighing less than 110 pounds.

The younger of my two sisters had become very fond of an old friend of our grandmother, our so-called Aunt Alice who was Jewish. In order to continue seeing the elderly lady, she had invented a touching "trick." She would put up her coat collar, holding on to it so as to give the impression to passersby that she was hiding her "Jewish star." For, as an Aryan, it was better not to be seen visiting a "Jewish House." Through her brother, a famous zoologist who had emigrated to the US earlier, Alice Neumann had several times received the required documents for her own emigration, but each time she had given them to someone else. She certainly saw what was happening in Germany; she had no illusions – she simply thought it was more important to give younger people who still had their entire lives ahead of them a chance to emigrate. When the Gestapo came to her apartment in 1942 to take her away, she excused herself, went to her bedroom and swallowed poison.

In Berlin alone, seven thousand people escaped being transported to a concentration camp by committing suicide. Seven thousand men, women, and children!

23

Our mother was worried about her son in Russia. She anxiously awaited each of his letters from the field, or any news from a comrade home on leave bringing regards from him, and she was overjoyed whenever he himself came home on leave. With time she had formed the habit of going every day to the chapel of the "Pink Sisters" in the nearby Convent Church of St. Gabriel. It consoled her and, as she herself said, it gave her a serene faith.

The stream of different visitors to our home on Westend Allee never let up. There are many names in the private papers as well as in the archived documents that are just names to me. But there are others that bring to mind the people themselves, and I can see them before me – either because I met them or because my mother described them so vividly.

I can "see" Mrs. M., the viola player who lived with us in hiding for a while. My mother, rather irreverently, nicknamed her "Moses" – one reason was that she really was like a kind of foundling, and another, because she looked so very unmistakably Jewish. And that's why our mother imposed on her what amounted to a prohibition on going out in the daytime.

Still, life went on as usual in our house. One afternoon we had an extra guest for tea. He was neither a Jew nor being persecuted for some other reason, and he asked her quite casually, "Mrs. M., do you still remember when we saw each other last? It was at a house concert by Mrs. W. That must have been a year ago."

My mother's knees turned to jelly – what if he had been the wrong sort of person and recognized the woman after all this time! It would have meant the end of the musician. "Berlin isn't some little village. Who would have expected something like this to happen?" My mother was upset. Still, it was really rather unlikely for her to ever offer a cup of tea to the "wrong" sort of person.

The constant air raids and the increasing destruction during this period occasionally made survival for illegals a little easier than before. For instance, the report that an entire police headquarters with its registration office and files had been bombed into rubble and ashes counted as one of the better pieces of information. More than once my mother was able to get a "certificate of being bombed out" for one of the "submarines." She would go to the appropriate office and say that a certain person named so-and-so had been bombed out of their house and had lost everything, even their priceless food ration coupons. She would then give the address of a house that had been destroyed and was located in the precinct of a police headquarters that had been bombed, so that no one could disprove anything she'd said.

That's how the violist obtained a legal food-rationing card with an official rubber stamp on it and was able to move on to another hiding place.

If necessary, the official stamps could also be forged. The way "little" people forged such things wasn't very complicated, but it did the trick. First you peeled a hard-boiled egg, rolled it once across a genuine stamp, and then transferred the impression by rolling it across the appropriate place on the desired document.

I found the following story in the Archive of the Center for Research on Anti-Semitism: The wife of one of the doctors at the Jewish hospital had to be gotten out of Berlin. It was absolutely necessary. Her destination was Vienna. This was one of those rescue actions in which several people were involved because it couldn't have worked otherwise. Each one of those participating in the rescue operation knew only a small part of the story. My mother was one of the links in this chain, but she never knew the real name of the woman. It was her task to write on a piece of paper: "Looking for woman to darn socks and mend clothes," to sign it: "Very busy mother," and give our address. She took this piece of paper, as had been agreed, and attached it to the thick trunk of a certain plane tree growing in front of our busy post office on Reichs Strasse. Back then many trees were festooned with such scraps of paper, and they were always surrounded by people reading the messages – the precursors of the "Looking For" and "Found" newspaper classified ads of a later time. Among the many things these little slips of paper might say were, for instance: "Looking for meat ration coupons, offering gabardine pants" or "Would like to exchange unworn men's shoes, size 46, for bicycle." The doctor's wife was supposed to go to the large plane tree, take the piece of paper, go with it to the house on Westend Allee, and ring my mother's doorbell. There was one essential precondition for such a transaction: Both parties had to have total trust in each other even though they had never met before. The woman came, stayed for a few days, and did actually help mend clothes. Just in case someone might have traced her, my mother – as always – had prepared an excuse. If anyone asked, she would pretend to be surprised and justify herself by saying: "How was I supposed to know that the woman is Jewish? I needed someone to darn the socks, and the woman was ready to do the work – I was overjoyed! Finding someone these days is hard – you don't ask them first for their identification papers!"

The first part of the operation went off smoothly. The next step was harder, for the woman needed identification papers. So after some intensive reflection, the generous Donata thought of giving her, she was the same age, her own identity card. She didn't feel quite secure about it, for she had already reported this document "lost" twice before, applying each time for a new one. But there seemed no better way out of the dilemma. And so they invented the following scenario. During the afternoon commuter traffic, Mrs. Helmrich would be on a certain platform at the busy Friedrich Strasse train station rummaging in her pocketbook. In the process she would "accidentally" drop her identity card and walk on, as if she hadn't noticed it. Meanwhile, the doctor's wife standing nearby, was to pick it up, and walk off in another direction. – And that's what happened.

After some time had elapsed, Donata went to the station agent to report the loss. "Well now, don't get so upset. I'm sure you'll get your identity card back," the friendly agent consoled the distraught woman.

"No, I'll never get it back," she moaned, "because I also had bread coupons and a ten-mark bill in the card holder."

"Well, then you're probably right – nobody would return such things these days. So you have to go to the police and have them make out a new one for you."

"All right then. So there's nothing to be done," she said meekly and asked the agents for a document certifying that she had come to see him and reported the incident.

At the police station they reproached her for her negligence and said she could pick up the new document in three months. Now the next scene was played out: Mother "acted hysterical" as she called it. She moaned saying that that was impossible, after all her husband was District Farmer in Poland; he was an important man, and he expected her to visit him. She got her way. But then, when after only two weeks, she came to pick up her brand new identity card, the officer looked her in the eyes and said, "Well, Mrs. Helmrich, here is the valuable card – but you have to promise me that you will never again – listen to me – never again lose it." My mother was certain that he'd seen through her act. But he said nothing else, and it wasn't necessary. She had understood him perfectly.

No one knows what happened after that to the doctor's wife, whether she switched the photo, or changed the name on the identity card, or when and if she got to Vienna – if that really was her destination. It would have been much too dangerous to try to find out. My mother only got a very brief message that the doctor's wife – and she really was the doctor's wife – had gotten away safe and sound.

24

The opinion and information published and broadcast in those times consisted of – how could it be any different? – propaganda, lies, and appeals to hold out. Anyone who wanted to know what was really going on in the world listened to "enemy" radio stations. This, of course, was strictly forbidden, and violators were punished. So it was important not to be caught doing it. The reception of the BBC German-language newscasts must have been pretty good, from a technical quality point of view, as well. At home, we listened to them on a daily basis – at very low volume. Often our mailman, Haibel, a socialist and passionate anti-Nazi, would join us for the ten o'clock news broadcast. Officially, he was having a cup of ersatz coffee so that his little "morning break" at No. 99f wouldn't raise suspicions. And he actually did drink his cup of ersatz coffee, but the more important thing for him was to get the unvarnished truth about what was going on in the world.

These BBC broadcasts began – I'll never forget – with the first four notes of Beethoven's Fifth Symphony, bam, bam, bam, baam! – his so-called Symphony of Fate. What an irony! Those four tones were not only a secret code of recognition for people "in the know," but they were also quite familiar to the Nazis and their informants. And so my mother thought she wasn't hearing right, when one day one of her (helpful) market women called out to her: "'Mornin', Mrs. Helmrich, heard the bam, bam, bam, baam today?" It scared my mother half to death, and she reproached the woman, but luckily the careless remark didn't have any further consequences.

It was customary to pass on the news from the British station via "mouth radio." Other important information was passed along the same way, from mouth to mouth. In my mother's circles people exchanged "reliable" addresses; you heard about other people who were ready to help and took down their phone numbers and you gave each other tips. It was a kind of oral Information Exchange.

No matter how hard you tried to be careful and discreet, and even though being constantly on the alert became second nature, there were always moments when something totally unforeseen could happen, moments of shock and fear when you couldn't be certain whether this time things would turn out well or whether it was all over.

One afternoon a young woman, a casual neighborhood acquaintance, came running over to see my mother and told her, gasping for breath, "For heaven's sake, go to Steuben Platz right away – your two 'Ukrainians' are sitting in the café there eating ice cream and chatting in their best Viennese dialect!"

"So I rushed over there as fast as I could," my mother said. She dragged the two girls – Susie and her sister Hansi from Drohobycz – out of the café and scolded them. She was beside herself, "You must have been completely crazy to do a thing like that!"

"But it was so beautiful," Susi said.

"Yes, I can believe that, but it might have backfired beautifully too!"

The two girls begged for forgiveness and promised to be more careful in the future. They never did it again.

After the war we found out that the young woman who had warned my mother had hidden her own best girlfriend in her apartment for two years, sharing the meager food rations with her.

For many years my mother had been friends with Edith, a Jewish woman from Hamburg who had moved to Berlin with her "Aryan" husband and daughter. Everything seemed to be going well – until the Gestapo found out that the young girl was not the biological daughter of Edith's husband, as he had claimed. Renate, that was the girl's name, was from Edith's brief first marriage to a Jewish man who had committed suicide.

After that things happened lightning fast. The Gestapo acted instantly, and they were already standing outside the front door ready to pick up Renate, when she jumped out of a rear window of their first-floor floor apartment and into the courtyard. She arrived at our place on the Westend Allee totally out of breath. She didn't stay with us for long, only a couple days.

Through the private resistance "Information Exchange" my mother had found out about a yachtsman who would be sailing to Sweden from Pichelsdorf, a Berlin district on the banks of the Havel River. A Mrs. Schmidt had been coming by our house several times after dark, suggesting to my mother that one of her protégés might escape on that yacht. She, Mrs. Schmidt, would arrange it. A date was mentioned, and it was agreed that Renate would be waiting down at the dock in Pichelsdorf at eight o'clock that evening.

Toward noon on the appointed day Donata started feeling uneasy. In the course of the afternoon she got cold feet. "All these years I risked my life doing the craziest things," she mused years later, "but back then I suddenly got terribly anxious and felt, 'There's something not quite right about this.'" And that evening, when the time came for Renate to leave, she said to her, "Don't go, stay here! Only over my dead body are you going to meet this yachtsman!" Renate did not go, and one or two days later they found out that the yachtsman had been apprehended, and none of the other people on board the boat were ever heard from again, nor Mrs. Schmidt either – if that really was her name.

"And you never found out which side she was on?" I asked my mother.

"No, no one knew, and it would have been unwise to ask." You really had to have strong nerves along with a good "nose" to sniff out danger, and lots of good luck.

It turned out that in the course of the remaining twenty months of war, Renate completed quite an adventurous odyssey.

From Berlin, using a false name, she went to mother's first husband and his family on the Darss Penninsula, where she worked as an officially employed mother's helper. When things in the small village seemed to get a bit dicey and they were afraid her true identity might be discovered, the twenty-year-old Renate returned to bombed-out Berlin. After that she lived the dangerous life of a hunted person with a false name and rather skimpy identification papers that would scarcely have held up under a close inspection. She lived with other young people who were either hiding from the Nazis or fighting them or doing both. These temporary friends helped each other as much as they could. They had to move frequently from one place to another, all the while organizing dare-devil rescue operations for others.

What is frequently ignored is that the persecuted Jews often took an active part in the fight for their own survival. The popular picture of active non-Jewish rescuers and passive Jewish victims obscures an important aspect of what was actually happening. These young people risked a great deal. They wanted to survive, to stay alive, and they also wanted to help others as much as they could, and they wanted to decide, in a very limited way, how to live their perpetually endangered lives.

One night Renate worked so hard helping to extinguish a fire in the house next door that the enthusiastic air raid warden nominated her for a medal (the *Kriegsverdienstkreuz* – Wartime Distinguished Service Cross) that honored extraordinary accomplishments by civilians. Tough luck for her! When she found out about it, she hastily and regretfully left her hiding place and fled to another section of Berlin.

Her next step was a remarkable challenge to fate: Renate registered for a course as foreign-language secretary – an incredibly daring idea but it also made sense. Even in the days when she was still called a "half-Jew," she hadn't been allowed to attend high school. Understandably she had a normal need "to get on with my life," as she wrote later in a letter from her new homeland. She just wanted to live and to do something with her time that would be useful to her later on too. Unfortunately the day arrived when a man from the Foreign Ministry came to the secretarial school to find a person to work in his department. And of all people, he chose Renate because she was the best in her class in English. Once again, she had to disappear head over heels and find another place to hide.

Not long after all the stress and the war was over, she left Germany. She enrolled as a university student, first in the United States, then in South America, finally ending up in England. She never returned to Germany.

25

In April 1992, I was invited to speak in several cities in the USA about Germany and its policies on foreigners and asylum-seekers. At that time not a day passed without reports of attacks on foreigners, homes of asylum seekers being burned, and screaming right-radicals going after defenseless civilians with baseball bats.

These happenings were watched abroad with great interest, especially on the East Coast of the United States. Perhaps people would be more likely to believe the German Government Representative for Foreigners – I held that honorary post at the time – when I told them that these images, terrible though they were, should not be equated with Germany and its citizens. Also – and this was not intended as an excuse – that racism was spreading not only in the German Federal Republic, but also in other European countries. And they seemed to accept that. Criticism of the indecisive and highly conflicting government policy was certainly in order, but it wouldn't be glossing over the facts to say that the great majority of Germans were horrified and worried by the daily brutality displayed towards foreigners.

The last event on that trip was the most awkward, and it presented a difficult obstacle course for me. I was supposed to speak at an interreligious ceremony on the occasion of Holocaust Memorial Day at the community synagogue in a small town in New Jersey, half an hour by car or train from New York. I wondered anxiously whether I would be able to find the right words. As the evening approached, my hands were ice-cold, I couldn't swallow a bite of food, and my legs seemed made of jelly. Here was this German politician, a member of the nation of criminals – most of the people in the audience must think of my appearance there

Cornelia Schmalz-Jacobsen, City Council member, Munich, second from left, 1978

as a sort of provocation. True, I was introduced with very kind words by a member of the congregation who pointed out that I was the daughter of "righteous gentiles," Christian rescuers of Jewish lives, but you could feel the tension in the room.

Back when I was a child in Berlin, I imagined that my parents, of whom I was so very proud, would survive the war and would be greatly admired, and we, their children along with them. That soon proved to be a pipe dream, for no one in Germany was interested in resistance to the Nazis and the rescue of persecuted people. Later I would have another reaction to add to that: Abroad, we, as Germans, were and remained representatives of the nation that had brought war, terror and murder to millions of human beings. At some point, it doesn't matter at all anymore to anyone (except to yourself) who your family was and what your father and mother did – even if, at the risk of their lives, they broke with their own country. As a German, you're one of them, and you can squirm this way and that, but all attempts to justify

The newly elected Senate of West-Berlin, April 1985. Cornelia, first row, fourth from right
Eberhard Diepgen, Mayor | Landesbildstelle Berlin

yourself are inappropriate and superfluous.

The wise phrase, "Collective shame" formulated by the first President of our country, Theodor Heuss, will keep its significance for many years to come. You find this out at moments such as the one I faced that evening in April.

And that's how I, the German speaker that evening, perceived the precariousness of my situation – full of uncertainty, dejection, and shame. But once I had concluded my talk and applause filled the hall, the leaden weights dropped from my shoulders.

No sooner was the official part over, then two well-dressed women about my age came toward me with outstretched hands. "So wonderful to meet you," they called out – a common American phrase, but in this case they really meant it. The two women had found out – to this day I still don't know how – that Eberhard Helmrich's daughter was coming to speak at this ceremony. They'd

Representative of the Federal Government for foreigners and refugees affairs, October 1992

gotten into their car and driven two hours to meet me. They told me that they were originally from Drohobycz, and how my father – "the most kind-hearted human being you can imagine" – had taken care of their families and that they owed their lives to him. They talked and talked. It was deeply moving; we embraced with tears running down our cheeks. I believe all three of us were very happy during those few minutes.

Only afterwards did I realize that we had forgotten to exchange addresses, and unfortunately, I also forgot the two women's names after this brief encounter. It's possible I didn't really "forget," but sensed instinctively that it was this moment of our meeting which mattered, and that it was a unique moment, and anything more would be insignificant.

Nevertheless, I remembered one name they had mentioned: Feit, Irene Feit. Remarkable that this was the only name I still remembered days later. It may have had something to do with my earlier work as a journalist. Back then I knew a woman with the same last name, and so the name itself was familiar. During the brief conversation at the synagogue I had found out that this Irene Feit, who lived in the US, had traced my father and that she had something to do with his being honored by the State of Israel.

I looked her up on the Internet, and after several phone calls to the "wrong" Feits, I found the "right ones" – Irene and Michael Feit in Highland Park, Illinois. She was surprised by the phone call from a stranger in Germany, but only for the first few seconds. Then the words just tumbled out. We talked, or actually, Irene talked, and I listened. She had met Eberhard Helmrich in Drohobycz – or should one say, she had "experienced" him? For she said right at the start of our conversation, "His kindness and warmth were unimaginable." Then, for a moment, she couldn't speak – she swallowed hard remembering this life-saving encounter during a dreadful time.

And so, little by little, Irene told me her story.

26

Irene Feit is a serious, calm, unflappable, white-haired woman. A middle-class American who lives with her family in comfortable circumstances. But she has to struggle to keep her composure whenever there is mention of those terrible three years in her life, after which nothing was as it had been before. Repeatedly she is kept from going on with her story by tears – the images and feelings from a time long gone by seem to be only the blink of an eye away. In seconds all the painful details come back. And they never stop being painful.

She had a wonderful, lighthearted childhood. Irene tries hard to describe to me the quiet and sheltered life she had. Her father, Dr. Leon Miszel, was the doctor who was working at the Jewish Hospital of Drohobycz when the Germans first occupied Poland. The food for his patients came from Eberhard Helmrich. She told me about her father.

Leon Miszel came from Stryj, a small village about thirty kilometers from Drohobycz. His wife Berta was from Western Poland. After studying medicine in Vienna – a time he struggled through together with his brother – the two brothers married two sisters and settled in their homeland. Leon Miszel moved to Drohobycz with his young wife because prospects in that "Polish Texas," with its peaceable, mixed population, seemed promising. In 1922, Halina their first daughter was born. Three years later, in July 1925, Irene was born. They lived in a beautiful house where the father also had his practice – they were doing well.

She wasn't raised with a real religious Jewish background, Irene said, because there was no Reform Judaism group in the town, and her parents felt they had nothing in common with

Hassidic Orthodox Jewishness. It was foreign to them.

Irene attended public school the first six years, after that she had to go to a private high school because there was no public girls' high school. This was the first time – she was twelve years old – that she experienced anti-Semitism in the attitude of her Polish classmates. Irene was flabbergasted. Suddenly she realized that the Miszels had been associating exclusively with other Jewish families.

After the war began and the Russians came, "it was still nice for us children because nothing had changed. In the summer we drove around in a horse and wagon, in the winter on a horse-drawn sleigh," she recounts. On the other hand, quite a few things changed for her parents: Russian soldiers were billeted in their house, and they had to squeeze into less space to make room for them.

The months went by, the German army was successful, and a feeling of growing uncertainty and anxiety about the future spread among the Jews. None of it really bothered the young people; they were having a good time. The Russians were friendly to them. "Besides, we were free in all respects," Irene recalls – perhaps a somewhat too rosy viewpoint – "and anyway, you don't want to believe that hard times are coming when you're young and happy." After Germany broke the Hitler-Stalin Pact and invaded the Soviet Union, the families in our circle of friends wondered whether it would be better to leave with the Russians or stay behind and wait to see what would happen. "We should all have left," Irene says, "but my parents decided to stay."

Yet it almost might have turned out differently, because the Russians simply took the doctor with them when they withdrew. But then, as soon as he was in the compartment on the train, he faked a heart attack. They let him go, and he quickly returned to his family in Drohobycz. There the situation for the Jewish population would change rapidly for the worse.

When the SS arrived, they requisitioned Leon Miszel's house

and closed down his medical practice

The family was able to find a new home, but sixteen-year-old Irene was not allowed to go to school, and her sister, who had begun studying medicine in Lemberg, had to leave the university. Halina had fallen in love there with a fellow student; they got married and moved to Drohobycz.

"In the beginning things were relatively all right," Irene recalls. "Because of my father's work we were somewhat protected. He worked in a hospital and he also treated German patients, and so we somehow got along." The family didn't have to live in the Ghetto, and Irene, along with other Jewish young people, was secretly given "private instruction" at home. They were taught by Jewish teachers who had lost their jobs at the school.

They lived from one day to the next; they made no plans. They knew what was happening all around them; that people were being randomly shot in the Ghetto, that anything the occupiers didn't like was met with severe punishment – "and punishment always meant punishment by death." And they knew that their situation would only get worse. Yet, they never imagined the dimensions of the horror that was awaiting them.

During the first winter of the occupation, a Pole came to see Dr. Miszel and implored him to see his wife who had pneumonia. The problem was that the woman lived outside the city and that Miszel, as a Jew, was not allowed to travel anywhere outside the city where he lived. Thinking it over briefly, he decided to obey his physician's oath and defy the rules of the German masters. He removed his Jewish star and drove with the Pole to see the man's sick wife. Most people bowed to the conditions laid down by the terror regime. But a few did not. As it turned out, the woman did get well, and his strictly forbidden patient-visit remained undiscovered.

In the fall of 1941 the Jews who lived in Galicia became convinced that they were doomed, that no one would spared. Many of them, Irene's parents among them, decided to do everything they could to save at least their children. Leon Miszel obtained "Aryan" identity cards for his two daughters and his son-in-law and distributed whatever money he still had left among them. The young couple went to Warsaw and were able to survive the war there. A job was found for Irene at a post office in Lemberg – but how was she to get there?

Doctor Miszel asked his "old acquaintance" Helmrich for help. And so my father arranged for a room in Lemberg that Irene could sublet under her fake identity, and his driver Janek Wojnar once again took on the role of people-smuggler, taking the young girl safely to her destination.

Irene was seventeen, and for the first time in her life, she found herself alone and having to shift for herself.

She immersed herself in the unfamiliar tasks. The workday was long, and there was little free time, which, in her solitude, she considered a blessing. As she sorted the mail, she noticed a strange smell that was always present and never seemed to let up. When she asked her post office colleagues about the odor, they told her that close by there was a crematorium that was in operation day and night. The infamous Lemberg Janowska Camp was not far away. "I can still smell it today. I've never been able to rid myself of it." Irene swallowed. "I know what it smells like when human beings are being burned."

At that time, she continued, she often visited a nearby Catholic church. "It was a good place to sit and cry without being disturbed."

It all went well for a couple of months. But one day at work Irene accidentally overheard a remark by an unfamiliar voice, "There's supposed to be a Jewish girl working here among you." She knew that they were probably talking about her, and so she fled as fast as she could to the train station. Luckily she still had a little of the money her parents had given her, and she was able to buy a ticket to Stryj where her uncle lived, from one of those "whisperers" – "Psst, do you need something? What can I get you?" She thought it would be too dangerous to go to back to Drohobycz. The wait for the train and the not really very long ride seemed to stretch on endlessly because Irene was in a panicky fear that she might be recognized as being Jewish. "The Germans weren't particularly good in that," she said, "but the Ukrainians were, and they were everywhere. And they were only too happy to help the Germans."

Irene was lucky and arrived safely at her relatives' home. But she couldn't stay there, and so her uncle immediately got in touch with the local Jewish Council, and they in turn informed Irene's parents of her whereabouts. Leon Miszel went to District Farmer Helmrich and asked him for help. In the meantime some things had changed for Dr. Miszel and his wife, too. Both had been transferred to a labor camp. Helmrich had been able to arrange for the doctor to help out at the first aid station there; he was of course no longer able to practice as a doctor.

Once more the Polish driver Wojnek was sent to get Irene. Helmrich had her brought to his apartment because, for the moment, it seemed the safest place for the young woman. He met her there for the first time, and as she's telling me about this first meeting, the tears run down her cheeks. "He shook hands with me and addressed me by name." She still can't seem to quite believe it all these years later. "Just imagine, this good-looking, elegant German actually shook my hand. And he spoke with me calmly and pleasantly." She said she wonders sometimes whether anyone today who hadn't lived under those conditions could imagine the moral value (she uses the word "value") this had then, when a German official of the occupying power treated a Jew with respect. "Suddenly I felt like a real human being again."

She stayed hidden in my father's apartment for two weeks. During that time he obtained new "Aryan" papers for her, and she worked for a short time as a Polish woman, always in danger of being discovered again. Then another miracle occurred: The

Polish farmer's wife who had been cured of pneumonia by Irene's father, asked whether there was anything she could do for Leon Miszel in return. The doctor asked her to hide his daughter from the murder commandos instead of himself and his wife. And so Irene was taken in secret to the house of the Kozlowski family. She described the poverty of the people and the generosity they showed her throughout the fourteen long months until the retreat of the German armies. "They treated me like a guest even though they knew very well that they would be put to death if I was found there." Irene stayed in their attic for the entire time. During that sad exile she started knitting sweaters and socks that her host family could sell. And she read anything the family could get for her. (Among other things, she read *Winnie the Pooh*, a book that she re-discovered many years later in a New York shop window after she had emigrated to the US.) The farmer's daughter was Irene's age, and she regularly brought her food and drink, "and she came regularly to get my chamber pot and empty it." It was rather embarrassing for her, but the girl did it with imperturbable pleasantness. "She could have gotten fed up and angry at me," Irene says, still marveling at it.

Throughout all these months Irene knew nothing about her parents and was afraid that they might no longer be alive. But they had managed to find a hiding place with some brave, sympathetic Poles. They stayed there, along with thirty-seven others like them, and were able to survive. To this date, 5,632 Polish rescuers have been nominated by those they rescued to be honored at Yad Vashem. By far the largest number from any single country.

A terrible time began right after the liberation for those who survived the Holocaust. They were caught between the fervent hope of seeing the familiar faces of family and friends again and the abysmal fear of not finding any of them alive anymore. They went in search of relatives. The Miszel family was one of the few where both the father and mother as well as the two daughters and son-in-law had survived the terror. All their other relatives, the parents' sisters and brothers and their families were gone, with one exception.

Irene recalls that many weddings took place in her parents' home after the war. For the survivors everywhere soon created new families. Her parents frequently served as witnesses to the marriages, because there were so very few families left intact.

Once the situation started getting back to normal – if one can even use such a word in this connection – Leon Miszel reopened his medical practice. The older daughter and her husband went back to the university, and Irene to school. "School was a joke; we learned practically nothing; they stuffed the material for two school years into one," she says. "But at least they awarded me my diploma."

After the initial joy of finding one another again, something really alarming happened, something quite unexpected. Irene told about being overwhelmed by a rush of crushing guilt feelings: Why did I survive, why didn't others instead of me? She talked about how the young people tormented themselves with reproaches: Why did we let it happen? Couldn't we have done something?

While the murders were going on it was different – at that time you looked at the world cynically: "They killed my girlfriend? Oh well, I still have a little breathing room – and tomorrow they'll drag me off! Another day won." Back then "luck" had a rather sarcastic interpretation: It was lucky if someone died suddenly, a second stroke of luck if someone was shot right then and there.

But now? Now they were the ones who'd escaped and survived, and they'd always remain the ones who survived. But the others – nobody could ever bring them back! Irene recalls how she started chain-smoking, one cigarette after the other, and how her contemporaries drank themselves into unconsciousness. By pure chance they had survived; others by pure chance had been killed – how could they cope with that?

The rest of the story was quickly told. Since they were Polish citizens, the Miszel family was given permission to leave the city of Drohobycz, which was now part of the Ukraine, and to settle anywhere in Poland, if possible in the former German districts. They moved westward, first to Gleiwitz, then farther on to Breslau (Wroclaw). But there was nothing to keep Irene in Poland. She did not believe that she and others like her had any future there. There had also been repeated anti-Jewish riots. She wanted to emigrate to America, and so, after she finished school, she went to Frankfurt to a camp for "displaced persons." She had to wait there a long time, because the US quota for Polish immigrants was small. She decided to make use of the time and enrolled at the university there. Uncomfortably, she remembers the many Germans who said they knew nothing about what had happened during the war. Most of them, however, immediately told her about their opposition to Nazism, and Irene says that sometimes she would try to embarrass these over-eager students by asking them, "Well, and where are all the Nazis now?"

In 1949 – the same year as my father – she was allowed to emigrate to the USA, where she then switched from one job to another. In 1956 she married Michael. He was a survivor from Tarnopol, which used to be part of Poland. They had two daughters. For a long time they didn't tell the girls anything about their past history. In 1958 they were able to bring Irene's parents over to the U.S., and later also her sister and her husband.

Irene had saved her 1942 *Arbeitsausweis* (labor ID card) as a spooky "souvenir." It was made out in German with a Swastika and the German eagle.

27

"Every survivor has a story about a miraculous rescue," Irene Feit once said. I've been told about many such miracles and read about them. It's hard to believe how different these stories are, one from the other, how touching, overwhelming, encouraging, crazy, or sometimes even hair-raising. They encompass the entire scale of courage, sympathy, quick-wittedness, and crazy ideas that the rescuers were capable of.

But back to Drohobycz and to 1941/42.

Both my mother and my father often mentioned the name "Backenroth." For a long time I didn't know whether he was a Jewish or an "Aryan" Pole. In my memory the name is connected with a person who was a "terrific fellow," a "hell of a guy." And my fantasies about this man weren't so far off, as I've found out in the meantime. He was actually Jewish, and he had the dubious task of acting as an intermediary between the Jewish Council and the Security Police. Naftali Backenroth, an engineer by profession, must have had a very stable disposition. He never allowed the unending horrors all around him to paralyze him; on the contrary, they seemed to mobilize his ingenuity and his energy. He tried to organize the *Judeneinsatz* (putting the Jews to work) in such a way that as many as possible of his Jewish protégés could have a better chance of surviving. Another goal he resolutely pursued was to interest the particularly brutal SS *Hauptscharführer* (Chief Squad Leader) Felix Landau in some relatively peaceful activities. This SS man, who was born in Vienna and was head of the Jewish labor effort, was in a way a member of the SS aristocracy and enjoyed a lot of liberties. In other words: He could follow his sadistic tendencies with impunity. What made him part of the "aristocracy" was the "Blood Order of the NSDAP" that the Nazis had awarded him. The description of the award makes you shudder – pictures of all the murdered people come alive. The meaning of the name, for the Nazis, was of course a different one, a shiny clean one, so to speak.

As early as the summer of 1941, this man was already taking part in the shootings of Jewish "intellectuals" in the Bronitz Forest. In his war diary, which was presented at the trial against him early in the sixties, Felix Landau describes his "going into action" like this:

"At 6 a.m. I am suddenly awakened from a deep sleep. Time to report for an execution. Oh well. and so I'm going to act as hangman and right afterward grave-digger, why not. It's really odd; you love fighting, and then you have to shoot down unarmed human beings. Twenty-three are supposed to be shot. Among them I find the two women I mentioned before. They are amazing. They refused to accept even a glass of water from us. I'm assigned as a marksman and have to shoot any who may try to escape. We drive along the road for a few kilometers and then turn right into a forest. For the time being there are just six of us. We look for a suitable place for the shooting and burial. After a few minutes we find an appropriate place. The doomed men arrive with shovels to dig their own graves. Two of them are crying; the others seem to be surprisingly brave.... The doomed men are divided into three shifts, since there aren't enough shovels. Strangely, I am not moved by this, I feel no pity – nothing – this is the way it is, and with that everything is settled for me.... The hole is gradually getting bigger. Two are crying uninterruptedly; I let them dig longer; that way they don't think so much. And while they're working they actually quiet down some. Valuables like watches and money are put into a pile. After all of them are bought to an open clearing nearby, the two women are the first to be stood up to be shot near one end of the pit. Two men had already been shot in the bushes by our Probationary Detective Superintendent (K.K.a.p.)…The women step up to the pit, calm and collected, then turn around. We had six men to shoot them. It was decided three would aim at the heart and three at the head; I chose the heart. The shots are fired and brain matter flies through the air. Two men shooting at the head is too many. They almost rip the head away completely. Almost all the victims sink down soundlessly. There are only two with whom it doesn't work, and they cry and whimper for a long time. Shots from our revolvers are ineffectual. The two of us shooting together don't miss. The next to the last group has to throw the previously shot people into the mass grave; then they have to stand up, and then they fall in on being shot. The last two have to sit on the rim of the grave pit so that they will fall in properly. Then a few of the bodies are moved around with a pick, and we start burying the dead. I come back dog tired, and now we go back to work putting everything in order in the building."

Thereafter, all the "shootings of Jews" from Drohobycz and the surrounding area took place in that forest. Landau in his diary calls it "*Übersiedlungen*" (removals), and they became routine. (This monster was arrested by the Americans in Linz in 1946, but he was able to escape from the internment camp. He lived under a false name, as an ordinary self-employed citizen in the German Federal Republic until 1958. In 1962 the Stuttgart District Court finally sentenced him to life imprisonment.)

Backenroth, the contact man, began by forming permanent work groups – salvation through work! He organized a handyman service and technical leadership for the new construction projects being constantly undertaken. That's how he got the idea of suggesting the construction of an indoor riding ring to the gentlemen of the SS. The idea struck a chord, especially with Landau. When the building was inaugurated in May 1942, his superior named him chief of the accredited agents in charge of the horses, and from that time on he was busy with riding lessons. And this, which seemed a rather grotesque example of black humor, was just a part of the everyday madness, but it was also part of Engineer Backenroth's circumspection. Soon there were about two hundred Jews working under his supervision at the various building projects. Jews who, as a consequence, were kept away from the death squads. At least temporarily. In addition, Backenroth managed to discover during that time new hiding places to be used when needed, and to convert and improve existing ones.

Backenroth must have been an impressive man – one who radiated authority and imperturbability. He was respected even among the Gestapo. But wasn't it too bad that this strapping man with the gleaming blue eyes was a Jew!

It was during this time that he and Helmrich met for the first time, and Backenroth in an interview later described what that was like. "One day – I was at work – the mayor of Drohobycz comes walking toward me, an old acquaintance, and with him is a tall, handsome German. That was Helmrich. He told me that he needed someone like me on his staff, and that he would pay the customary wage. I answered, 'I'm sorry, but I'm employed as a forced laborer, and if I go to work for you, I'll be considered a collaborator.'

He looked at me in a funny way then and said, 'What are you talking about?' – and at that instant I knew that he was a good man." That day an official employer-employee work relationship was agreed on. But above and beyond that, a deep friendship developed between the two men; they knew that they could trust each other completely and their secret, mysterious "teamwork" to save the persecuted was based on this mutual trust. They told each other everything worth knowing, and Helmrich was often able to warn the engineer of impending "actions." In their boldness, their sober reflection, and their readiness to help, these two must have been soul mates, kindred spirits. With the passage of time,

Backenroth came to know about fifteen different safe hiding places, and he saved the lives of many people. Among those he saved was his nephew Emmanuel Weintraub who lives in Paris today and told me about it.

Yet in spite of the power of his position, and despite his considerable presence of mind, Naftali Backenroth's situation was becoming increasingly more dangerous. "We have to do something. We have to think up something we can do for you; it can't go on like this," his friends would tell him, and perhaps he was thinking the same thing.

The idea that saved him sounds absolutely incredible, but it was implemented. A really audacious, madcap scenario was devised – no one can remember who thought it up, but possibly it was an idea the group had worked out together.

In any case, in the spring of 1943 a rumor suddenly started circulating that Backenroth wasn't Jewish. Unfortunately the story was a very embarrassing, rather slanderous one, which no one who knew it wanted to talk about.... After a reasonable amount of time the myth was finally revealed: In 1905, Backenroth's mother was delivered of a baby boy in a Lemberg clinic. Unhappily the infant was too weak and died right after birth. The mother didn't know about the baby's death, and the poor, stricken father didn't dare tell his wife the terrible truth. At that point, kind fortune presented them with an answer that was wonderful in every way. For, only a few rooms down the hall, a poor, unmarried "Aryan" serving girl had also given birth to a boy, a healthy one. But the poor girl, what was she to do? She couldn't keep this child of shame. What was going to become of her and her poor child! A scoundrel, a skirt chaser known all over the city – "Aryan" of course – had made the poor girl pregnant. Such things used to happen often. So what could be more obvious than, let's say, making both women happy? So they put the serving girl's baby into the arms of the unknowing Mrs. Backenroth, and everything was all right. Except that, unfortunately, after thirty-eight years, the matter had now come to light as the result of an indiscretion.

To make the comedy believable, an "old-style" birth certificate was produced and they found a doctor – whom they bribed – who confirmed with his signature and official stamp the exchange of babies back then. The Gestapo swallowed the story hook, line, and sinker and gave a little party for the new-born "Aryan" – after all, they'd known all along that he couldn't be a Jew – "You with your blue eyes!"

One of them, though, didn't quite believe it. He asked Backenroth for a blood sample and sent it to the *Rassenhygiene* (Racial Hygiene) Institute in Berlin. This humbug institution immediately sent back the reassuring news that the blood was "quite all right." Thereupon Backenroth legally and officially changed his name. From then on it was "Bronicki."

In 1944, when the Germans were withdrawing, his "friends" in the Gestapo said, "And you'll come along with us!" Thereupon he hid in a place where they couldn't find him. He stayed on in Drohobycz. Then, when the Soviets invaded, just for a change, they arrested him. But they let him go again soon afterward. Following some back and forth, a series of annoying obstacles, and some lucky accidents, Backenroth/Bronicki was able to emigrate to France with his family. His son, Lucien, a man of about my age, whom I met at the tree planting for my mother, now lives as a successful businessman in Israel.

The father died peacefully quite a number of years ago. Right after the Second World War this remarkable man from Drohobycz, Galicia, had decided to make the name change permanent. And he took the name "Bronicki" for himself and his descendants. That name was to be a reminder of the Forest of Bronitza where most of his relatives and many thousands of other unlucky victims were murdered.

28

In those days, being able to work was a matter of life and death for the victims of Nazi persecution. The first to be killed were the "dispensable or superfluous Jews" – that was the officialese term for it! It referred to the old, the sick and weak, children, and many women. For that reason the victims fought hard and stubbornly for any chance at all of a job. No wonder bribery and corruption flourished.

Or the occupying forces would set arbitrary quotas for "extermination": twelve hundred Jews – three thousand Jews – five thousand Jews – just like that. Part of this scheme was the forced participation of the Jewish Councils; any kind of refusal to go along was out of the question. Some on the Council entertained the illusory hope of being themselves spared, and went about their assignments assiduously and with no less brutality than their taskmasters. The Head of the Jewish Council of Borislav was in the end killed by his own people in an act of revenge. Backenroth wasn't able to back out when Felix Landau, bearer of the Blood Order, took him along to the train station and forced him to help "load" the victims collected for "transportation" into the waiting freight cars. He *had* to do it or face death, like all the many others.

For reasons no one could explain, seemingly at random, between the waves of violence, there were pauses in the "relocation" during which people started to breathe again. It would be no exaggeration to suggest that the Nazis' program had elements of improvisation, contradictions, even chaos. Ghettos were set up, but then not carried to completion. There was general dissension and disagreement within the local German leadership about whether they still needed "Work Jews" for the armament industry or whether they should do away with the whole slave labor effort. Even when, by 1943, there could no longer be any doubt that all Jews without exception were to be exterminated, there were still some exceptions.

There are shocking records that bear witness to the radicalization of the persecution of the Jews in Galicia and the complete brutalization of the perpetrators there. Among the many incomprehensible stories in this connection is the following incident, confirmed by other Germans:

The district leader of the NS women's group had requested permission for her group to attend a shooting of Jewish women. And the Nazi women actually came to the execution wearing their Mother's Crosses for the occasion. After that, having witnessed the shooting, what went through their minds while they were bathing their own children, dressing them, or when they were taking care of or nursing their own mothers or sisters?

In the face of the unremitting killings taking place within everyone's view, more or less publicly, the many efforts of people like Eberhard Helmrich must look rather ridiculous and insignificant. It wasn't always just a matter of saving a life, but often it was also about small things that for a brief moment gave dignity back to the oppressed and badly treated victims. Helmrich lent a hand and intervened wherever it seemed possible to him. Cautiously, unflinching, and often spontaneously.

One of the survivors, Dr. Joseph Weissmann, says that there were at least four occasions when he would have been grabbed on the streets of the Ghetto by the Gestapo, but that each time "Major Helmrich" got his persecutors to release him with the argument that he had urgent need of this outstanding expert on his vegetable farm. In reality, Weissmann was a doctor, but Helmrich with the help of a not quite truthful labor identity card simply appointed him "an agricultural expert." It was something he did often – a practice that belongs in the chapter "Rescue by

Means of Work" – turning people into "specialists" in all sorts of departments and sectors, even though their real professions were something else entirely.

Once Helmrich had hidden Joseph Weissmann and his wife for thirty-six hours in his own apartment until they were no longer in danger. Another time Helmrich was sitting in the barbershop getting a shave when, looking out the window, he happened to see two Ukrainians beating up Weissmann because he had been guilty of stepping up on the sidewalk, something Jews were forbidden to do. Helmrich stormed out into the street, his face still lathered up, yelled at the two Ukrainians, and chased them off.

In the fall of 1943, shortly before one of the last major "actions," Weissmann asked Helmrich for "Aryan" papers for himself and his family. But it was no longer possible to get these papers. Helmrich suggested that the doctor go into hiding since the war wouldn't last much longer anyway. At that time, the front was coming closer and closer, and in two, at most, three months, he thought, the Germans would be withdrawing from the area. This turned out to be wishful thinking, for the German forces managed to push the Red Army back one more time.

Weissmann and the nine members of his family went into a small, narrow subterranean hiding place that had been dug out of the ground. They could hardly stand up or move around, and there was barely enough air to breathe. They had to relieve themselves in the same space. The two or three months turned into three quarters of a year. During that time Helmrich saw to it that the family at least had food to eat and water to drink – more than that he could no longer do for them.

Once the German occupation forces withdrew, the Weissmann family, almost blind by then, crawled out of their hiding place into the light of day. Weissmann's mother didn't survive the time in the hole in the earth. She had died. Although surrounded by her family, they were unable to help her because of their predicament. They buried her right there in the loose earth. They had no choice.

At some point during the last months of the horror, when it was already obvious that the war on the Eastern Front was lost, Helmrich made another of his daring attempts to organize an escape abroad. He wanted to help his friend and coworker, Dr. Mauricy Ruhrberg and other members of the Jewish Council of Drohobycz to escape to Hungary. Their escape, however, failed. Ruhrberg was captured and shot.

The three-year German occupation had begun with mass executions and it ended with a final mopping up of all Jews. As late as 1944 they were still feverishly deporting them; the Gestapo hunted down hidden Jews; they liquidated Russian war prisoners as well as German and non-German rescuers whom they caught treating the persecuted victims humanely and sympathetically. The master race then held a "harvest feast" –which is what they called one of their most horrific operations – where they killed off everything and everyone they could kill in the slaughter-house that was Galicia.

Helmrich felt disheartened and worn out, and it troubled him that he had so few possibilities of helping anyone. He became ill and caught pneumonia. His condition improved somewhat once he was at home again in Berlin. Then he went back into Hell, to Drohobycz to attend to his position as District Farmer. And also to supply the hidden escapees with food.

In April 1944, Russian bombs dropped on Lemberg and Drohobycz. They didn't cause a great amount of destruction, but for the persecuted and those in hiding they heralded a turning point. "For us these were the fanfares of freedom," one of them later told me, "The sound of the bombs was the voice of Life!" And he said they clung to their conviction that these were good bombs and were not intended to harm them.

Nevertheless, the freight trains kept on rolling to the Krakau-Plaszów concentration camp. The "gathering up of Jews" was meticulously carried out and bureaucratically recorded.

Bureaucratic is also the word that describes the last situation report Helmrich signed and handed in. It was dated April 25, 1944. I discovered it in Lemberg at the Ukrainian Central Archive. In dry, official language it reports on the condition of the sowed crops, the feeding of cattle and pigs, about poultry flocks and bee-keeping, and in it the authorities in charge are informed to the smallest detail about the gathering of all kinds of agricultural products. All this sounds spookily unreal, as if people were living locked up in an insane asylum and wanted to prove to those on the outside that they were completely normal. Still, under the heading "General," I did find a few critical comments. There is mention of "The Mood in the Villages" and it points out that the inhabitants were suffering a lot because of encroachments by units of the German Army. It says, literally, "The units of the O. T. (*Organisation Todt*), the Wehrmacht, and the police which had remained in the rural area, in general do not contribute to the establishment of peaceful conditions there, but rather are a constant source of marketing disruption."

At another place, the document refers specifically to the "well-integrated non-German personnel who have proved successful in every way and deserve the highest praise."

The German occupation forces disappeared in the summer of 1944. Quite a few of the butchers made off and took on new identities. For the people of East Galicia August 6th became the long hoped-for day of liberation from the Nazi yoke.

Eberhard Helmrich went back to Berlin but remained there only a brief time. He was relieved to find out that bombs had destroyed our police station along with all its files. That would make it so much more difficult for the henchmen to find those who had escaped. Just to be sure he decided to disappear from

Berlin and move to Hamburg, the city of his childhood and youth. He was forty-five years old and was fed up – he didn't want to be involved, to take part in anything at all anymore. When Donata was asked by officials where her husband was, she answered coolly: "How should I know. Maybe he deserted me – who knows in these times!" After the last of the Nazi positions still holding out capitulated, she simply said, "I knew that he was in Hamburg, but I'm not crazy enough to hand my husband over to the *Volkssturm* (the German Territorial Army)!"

So that was the end of the Drohobycz and Galicia chapter.

Citing the numbers of the murdered victims may document the horror of "the Final Solution" in this area, but it cannot really give you a picture of the catastrophe. The painstaking records kept by the perpetrators of how many Jews there still were at any particular time, or tables listing various causes of death – "shootings, hunger, and disease, mass shootings and pogroms, deportations, mass deportations, 'Jew hunts' in the forests" – sketch a picture both conceivable and inconceivable. It always seems easier to imagine "lambs on the slaughtering block" than to think of individual human beings. To think of people who were completely at their mercy and had almost no chance.

There are some actual stories that give us an inkling of the nature and the extent of the crime. In Galicia alone, more than half a million people were killed – five hundred thousand names, five hundred thousand faces – extinguished.

Most of their murderers survived the war and internment. Only a fraction of them were put on trial after shamefully belated investigations.

29

The infamous Wannsee Conference on "The Final Solution to the Jewish Problem," January 20, 1942, was not the beginning of the end, because that had occurred quite a few years earlier; no, it signaled the end of the end. It was there that they set the course for the extermination of European Jews and also discussed the subject of including "Jewish half-breeds" and Jewish partners in "mixed marriages." From that day on, no more doubt could exist about the goal the National Socialists planned to achieve as mercilessly and quickly as possible.

But since they could not transport and kill all the Jews overnight, they thought up additional annoyances and constraints to impose on them while the "Jewish cleansing action" was being completed. Such as:

February 10, 1942, announcement that in Berlin no more firewood could be supplied to Jews who had "Coal Cards."

March 24th, Jews were specifically forbidden to use public transportation. Exceptions were allowed for school children and employees of Jewish establishments and slave laborers who had to travel more than seven kilometers to work. Only Aryans had the right to sit down. The journalist Ursula von Kardorff wrote in her *Berlin Notes* about a brief flash of bitter resistance and human solidarity: A worker made room so that a Jewish woman wearing the "star" could sit down, saying, "Sit down, you old star biddy." When a party member reprimanded him, he replied briefly, "Up my ass, fuck you all!"

On March 26th the Gestapo ordered that all Jewish apartments in all the German territory be marked with a white paper "Jew star."

On May 9th the Berlin Jewish Community was ordered to

make known that all of Unter den Linden, Tauentzien Strasse, and a part of Kurfuerstendamm were forbidden to Jews.

On May 15th Jews were forbidden to keep house pets. All their animals must be registered for collection by May 20th.

Three weeks later Berlin Jews were ordered to turn in without compensation "all clothing not essential for a modest lifestyle." (What was left then? Since the beginning of the war they had had no chance to buy new clothes, and all fur coats had been collected earlier.)

At the same time Jews were also ordered to hand over to the German State any optical or electrical appliances they owned, like binoculars, cameras, heat lamps, hot plates, vacuum cleaners, even typewriters and bicycles – without being entitled to any compensation.

On June 20th, they announced that within ten days all the Jewish schools, which had been set up since 1939 as a system separate from the other schools, were to be shut down. Students fourteen years or older were to report to the labor office for forced labor.

On June 6, 1942, the first deportation train left Berlin for Theresienstadt.

On July 11, the first deportation from Berlin direct to Auschwitz took place.

The proponents of the final solution had set the end of 1942, beginning of 1943, as their target date for the completion of the deportation of all full Jews from the Reich territory. In a few of the large cities, especially Berlin, the process took longer than planned. Many of the Jews marked for deportation had in the meantime chosen illegality and were living in hiding or under a different identity as so-called "submarines" or "u-boats." The wave of "going underground" reached its high point in the second half of 1942, for by now even the most naïve and trusting realized where – in the word's most terrible meaning – the journey was headed.

"The Final Solution" was subject to strict secrecy; yet in spite of that the belief that it was about "resettlement" or *Arbeitseinsatz* (labor assignments) was crumbling even among the German population. Too many of those who spent time in the Eastern territories – whether as members of the army or as civilian employees – knew what was going on there, and so a lot of information about the murder machinery in Poland made its way back to Germany. Also, some of the perpetrators, even though sworn to silence, had talked about their "work" while on home leave.

In a large city like Berlin with a high contingent of soldiers who had been called up or were on home leave, you would have had to be living on the moon not to have heard or seen anything! Did this knowledge have any effect on the attitude or behavior of the population? Did it encourage opposition to the Third Reich, maybe even promote a willingness to help the persecuted victims? Unfortunately we can only speculate about this. So far it is a blank spot in the historical research.

Reichsführer SS Heinrich Himmler wanted the deportations from Germany to be concluded by the end of February 1943. A nationwide raid was planned under the name *Fabrikaktion* (Factory Action), but information that a new blow against the Jews was being planned leaked out in time. The forced laborers were warned by their colleagues at work, by their bosses, foremen, regular employees, and engineers and even by some policemen and SS people at their work places. Thousands didn't go to work on February 27th or hid. In Berlin one out of every three of those the SS or Gestapo had in their sights were able to escape being deported. Nevertheless, in the German capital, some eight to ten thousand Jews were arrested at munitions factories, in offices, on the street, or in their apartments and interned in various "collection camps" for several days until their deportation.

It was said that Himmler wanted to present the Führer a Reich capital "cleansed of Jews" as a gift for his birthday on April 20th. There is no way of finding out whether this was true or merely a rumor.

During the "Factory Operation" a large number of Jews who lived in mixed marriages and many Jewish "half-breeds" were also grabbed, arrested, and locked up. For the most part these were men. They were housed separately from the "Full Jews" at Rosenstrasse 2-4. What were the Nazis planning to do with them? The prisoners and their relatives probably expected they would be deported and killed. According to more recent research, they were to be sent to fill the workplaces from which the "Full Jews" had just been taken. Whatever was planned for them, the food situation, the extremely crowded conditions, and the hygienic situation at Rosenstrasse must have been horrendous. The confusion and chaos as well. The others, the "unprotected" Jews, were taken first to the Grosse Hamburger Strasse and from there were shortly deported to Auschwitz.

The fate of the so-called privileged ones, however, took an unexpected turn. Many hundreds of "Aryan" relatives of the imprisoned Jews, mostly their wives, assembled outside on the street and demanding the release of the prisoners. They refused to be discouraged; taking turns, they would go home for short periods, but they didn't leave, staying on the spot for days on end. "The Women of the Rosenstrasse," as they were later called, organized the first and only mass protest against the extermination policies of the Nazis, and they were successful. In spite of repeated efforts on the part of the Nazis, they were not able to get the protestors to give up. What were the Nazis to do – shoot at German women? Inconceivable! Whether their superiors gave in or they had intended all along only to "intern" the "protected" Jews and not to deport them – between the 6th and 8th of March almost all of them were released.

This successful resistance action is mentioned by the journalist Ruth Andreas Friedrich in her writings, published originally in 1947. But except for her, no one seemed to be interested in taking up this exemplary and encouraging episode and to spread the news of it. On the contrary, information about it was suppressed and the episode was soon forgotten. No doubt it was their extraordinary courage and above all their success that people didn't like being reminded of. It would only have raised uncomfortable questions, which the majority of collaborators and those who had turned a blind eye didn't want to ask. Not until the late eighties was the story of the Rosenstrasse Protest rediscovered and made public by the American Nathan Stoltzfus.

30

Donata and her family went on living their risky lives as before, only now the conspiratorial community she was part of was moving ever closer together. They were keeping each other constantly informed of the latest developments, and a bed for any secret surprise guests was always ready.

One year after the end of the war, Donata made up a list of the people she had been close to during the Nazi years in friendship and through joint rescue actions. The list included two-hundred-thirty names, and many of those listed were plagued by the Nazis because they lived in "mixed marriages" or for other reasons. These people came from quite differential income levels. There was a "half-Jewish" doctor who had lost his position in a Berlin hospital; an actress whom the Nazis forbade to act on stage because she was suspected of leftist activities; a woman neighbor who was sentenced to ten months of prison after she was denounced for listening to "enemy" broadcasts; an upholsterer from Preussen Allee who wasn't afraid to help persecuted people; the police sergeant at the 123rd District who warned "his" people when an action was imminent, and many others. What they had in common was their hatred of the regime and the firm resolve to help those in need and to support one another.

There were also three couples on the list next to whose names it says: "illegally married." Jews and "half-Jews" were not permitted to enter "mixed marriages" at that time. They were not allowed to go to the Registry Office. Couples who wanted to legalize their union before God and receive a priest's blessing found clergymen who would marry them in secret. These marriages were not registered officially.

My mother must have hosted at least one such wedding ceremony in our home on Westend Allee, for she later mentioned that she had managed to get a "black" tongue for the festivities. This meant that on the menu for the wedding feast was a beef tongue she had acquired on the black market. No doubt the other ingredients came from mother's allies at the weekly market. An illegal piece of meat for an illegal wedding – entirely appropriate! After the war the couple remedied the lack of legality at the Registry Office. But the happiness and joy they experienced at their "black wedding" probably far outshone their feelings during the later bureaucratic procedure.

There were times when Donata's loyalty and unconditional willingness to help were sorely tested. A friend, a singer, had taken temporary shelter in her home after an air raid had damaged the place where he had been staying. Since neither he nor his friend wanted to join the army, they drank rancid oil, literally under Donata's eyes, in order to simulate jaundice – apparently quite persuasively. My poor mother! Sick with worry about her own son, who had to endure God-only-knew what hardships in Russia, and here she was confronted by two healthy men who were willfully doing harm to their health. It really troubled her because it was in such sharp opposition to her principles.

I can still remember exactly how sensitive she was when someone was pretending to be sick, because she considered this an impermissible provocation of fate, and was sure that fate would take revenge. As school children we could never ask her for an excuse from classes – not in our family! One didn't do things like that.

Another temporary guest – not someone in hiding, but a normal visitor – couldn't stop criticizing his hostess for a thousand trivial things. When he was confronted about this he'd say "*Wes' Brot ich esse, des Lied ich nicht singe!*" ("He who pays the piper doesn't call the tune.") – a perversion of the old saying. This stubborn self-righteousness hurt her more than any criticism. It's hard to understand why she didn't simply show people like this – who were just exploiting her generosity - the door. It probably had something to do with her conviction that the few decent and reliable people couldn't let each other down. Personal annoyances and hurt feelings were secondary.

31

In the fall of 1943, the nightly air raids were getting steadily worse, both in number and in intensity and destructiveness. After one fearful night I came to a decision. I had been left behind in the air raid shelter in the garden, dead tired, afraid, and silent. The adults had gone to help the neighbors put out fires. Actually, I wasn't alone in the shelter. What made the situation worse was that there was a young girl cowering across from me, ceaselessly screaming and praying. Her crying and wailing made me more afraid than the hissing and crashing of the bombs. My only consolation was her German shepherd dog, and I clung to him for safety.

Once the night came to an end and I was allowed to return to our house, I told my mother in no uncertain terms, "I want to get out of here!" And I knew where I wanted to go. I wanted to go to the Darss, to stay with Uncle Friedel and his family. My mother, probably to gain some time, said hesitantly that she would think it over. I'd only met Uncle Friedel that summer, and immediately felt a great fondness for him. In fact I reproached my mother for not having introduced this nice relative to me before.

Well, frankness about the political situation, the burden of imposed silence, and the responsibility of dealing correctly with being different from the others – that was one thing. It was quite another thing to reveal the truth about family relationships. Even in those crazy times there were things that I was still too young to hear! Because Uncle Friedel was actually mother's first husband. Dr. Friedel Greiff was the father of my sisters and brother. But I wouldn't learn about that for more than a year yet. No wonder mother had reacted so hesitantly, for she and her former husband had only recently established contact again.

Then a small miracle occurred. About half an hour after my announcement that I was going to the Darss, even before my mother had time to think up an excuse, the phone rang, and on the other end of the line was Uncle Friedel asking whether it wouldn't be better if Cornelia were to come to stay with them in the country. It must have taken a load off my mother's mind. I wasn't particularly surprised, for I was quite convinced in my heart that my decision would be turned into reality. I hadn't doubted it for a second.

And so, a few days later, in the second half of November, I went to the Baltic Sea. My mother couldn't come with me. Either she had no time or because it seemed that a meeting with her former husband and his present wife at this time was too abrupt. For that reason she asked an old friend from her youth in Weimar to take me to my destination. The train ride from the Stettiner Train Station in Berlin Mitte northward was unforgettable for me. We travelled through a destroyed city. It was in ruins, much worse than anything I had seen where we lived in Westend. In a way, this trip opened my eyes, and for the first time I began to have an idea what "war" meant.

We changed trains in Stralsund, then again in the little town of Barth. From there the train went to Zingst/Darss, which back then had only a small station. We were picked up by a horse-drawn cart that took us five kilometers on a country road to the village of Müggenburg in complete darkness. This small village with no more than a handful of houses was going to be my new home for the next two years and eight months. My family now consisted of Uncle Friedel, his wife, Aunt Maria, and their four-year-old son, Christian.

I was in completely different surroundings than I had ever known before. Uncle Friedel, who was actually a political economist by profession, and his wife had a farm with cows, horses, pigs, and poultry. They had a tractor and a big barn full of farm machinery. A country road connected the different villages on the peninsula. Our village had only one street, and we lived at one end of it. At the other end was the school. I had to get used to the new school too, for it was what later would be called a *Zwergschule*, a one-room school. All the grades up to the eighth year were taught in one room and by one teacher. My third grade consisted of three children. Some grades were temporarily without pupils because there were no children of that age, and in spite of that, amazingly enough, we were taught enough so that I was later able to move directly into high school in Berlin.

I hated the local history and geography lessons. Inevitably each lesson began with the pupils having to recite the sentence: "My homeland is Müggenburg in the Zingst District on the Darss Penninsula." But my homeland was not Müggenburg but Berlin, and so I refused to repeat the sentence. After a short time of being given the order and disobeying it – "You're going to repeat it in spite of that!" and "No, I won't because it's not true!" – a compromise was reached. I didn't have to speak about "homeland" anymore, but could instead say: "I live in Müggenburg...."

During that time I wasn't the only city child in the area, for other mothers had sought shelter in the country with their children. One of them was Aunt Hilde from Berlin-Zehlendorf, Uncle Friedel's sister.

There were good things and bad things about being in such a completely different environment. I felt terribly homesick and wrote tearful letters home. And every time large fleets of bombers flew over us in the direction of Berlin, I was filled with dreadful anxiety. I wasn't anxious about us "Müggenburgers" – they weren't going to drop any bombs on us, I knew that full well, but I was afraid for my mother, for my sisters, and for Hedda. After all, on the ride here I had seen what could happen. With those scenes of the destruction in my native city, I could easily imagine that Westend Allee might soon look like that too.

Clearly among the good things were the unaccustomed freedom of movement – the animals, the barn, playing up in the hayloft. I learned to swim in the Baltic Sea, and to ice-skate on the bay, an inland body of water. High points were the visits to Kirr, a little island in the bay whose only residents were Aunt Maria's parents, who had a farm there. The old house in the middle of an enchanted peasant garden, full of flowers, and protected from the wind by a thick boxwood hedge, seemed to me like Paradise. The inhabitants, Oma and Opa Bussert, may have contributed a good deal to this impression. They were kind, good-humored people who loved children. In the winter, when the ice was solidly frozen, you could reach Kirr on ice-skates; at other times, you could row over in a boat. When you were on Kirr, nothing could happen to you, that's how safe you felt there. To my child's mind it was a protected spot where fear could not enter.

Another of the good things about my new neighborhood was that it also had something like a conspiratorial group of people opposed to Hitler. But the pressure not to say anything outside the home was a lot less than it had been in Berlin. This was because "outside" was a lot smaller, and the likelihood of being caught saying a wrong word or listening to enemy radio stations was considerably less. It was definitely a relief for me. In my extended family they spoke quite openly. Also they didn't hesitate to speak openly in front of the two Polish servants, Sophie and Marianne. They were so-called *Ost-arbeiter* (workers from occupied countries like Poland, etc., who were forced to work in Germany), but I didn't know that at the time. Looking back I can't remember ever hearing any Nazi propaganda from our teacher or singing any Nazi songs.

Once when a pitiful, bedraggled group of men were being led, or rather driven down our country road, everybody talked about it, and as far as I can remember, with obvious sympathy for those poor boys. They were Russian war prisoners. I know nothing about where they came from or where they were being taken – in any case, there was no camp in the vicinity.

Now and then a black car would drive into the farmyard and a man in a brown uniform would get out. This was "Mueller" with his chauffeur. Mueller was a bigwig. He would salute sharply with "Heil Hitler" and have a conversation with Uncle Friedel. Then he would apparently look around the farmyard. While he was stomping around the property in his shiny black riding boots, Uncle Friedel would speak to him as if in a foreign language. And we children would clear out. Everyone was happy when he got back into his official coach and drove off. We made fun quite openly of the pompous man and his his pretentious way of speaking. We children and the Polish women aped the way he spoke. He didn't just call himself "Mueller" but laid stress on having everyone pronounce the "e" in his name separately: Mr. Mueller.

32

At our home on Westend Allee it was customary for guests to sit at the big table in the dining room for the midday dinner. The more the old customs were endangered, the more we came to appreciate them. No war, no bombs, no food rationing could spoil Donata's joy in having company.

One sunny Sunday morning in the summer of 1944, some good friends phoned, a young couple she had invited for dinner that day. They asked whether they might bring along a friend, a doctor who was in Berlin on a two-day furlough from the front.

"Of course, bring him along," was her spontaneous and probably expected reply. There was going to be a black-market leg of lamb with tomatoes. That would easily accommodate an additional guest.

Shortly before the meal, Donata looked out the window and couldn't believe her eyes: On the lawn next to her friends stood a young man wearing an SS uniform. They hadn't rung the bell but had simply walked into the garden from the street – that's why Donata hadn't noticed them before. She practically flew outside. The couple introduced the stranger, a doctor with an old German aristocratic name. And the conversation went something like this:

Donata, fuming with anger: "Unfortunately I must tell you, Count H., that you put me into a dreadful position. I swore that no one wearing your uniform would ever get even a grain of salt in my house."

The unbidden guest: "But my dear lady, please let me explain...."

Donata: "There's nothing to explain!"

He: "But please, one moment..."

She: "If I tell you where my husband has been District Farmer for three years – he's in Galicia – then will you still want to explain something?"

He: "But there are…."

She: "No, there aren't! If you were the son of a rag picker, then maybe there'd be something to explain. But as Count H. you really ought to know something about decency and good manners and one's proper place!"

Even years later she was still indignant: "In our clean garden, that black SS uniform – I thought I was going to go out of my mind."

The couple tried to assure her that "he really wasn't like that." But it didn't placate her. Anyone else would probably have reported Donata, but this uninvited guest had the decency not to do that.

33

Perhaps it was a lucky coincidence that just at that moment no "unofficial" guests were staying in the house. A state of affairs that never lasted very long.

A short time after the experience with the SS doctor there was again a surprise overnight visitor. One day when Donata came home exhausted from shopping – a laborious, time-consuming chore during those years – our faithful Hedda told her that Dr. R., his name was on mother's list too after the war, had been there with a lady who had a pressing need to go to Southern Germany and required documents. The lady would come back again later. Donata was not looking forward to meeting the strange lady. She had no more papers left from Drohobycz, and starting that game with the lost identity card all over again seemed too risky just then.

The door bell rang, and before her stood a woman who looked directly at her and said, "Donata – I'm Andrea!" She hadn't quite finished speaking when the two women fell into each other's arms. Once Donata recovered from the shock and they, I assume, were having a cup of tea in the living room, Andrea told Donata that she was fleeing from East Pomerania and wanted to reach her sister Vally in Munich. Andrea was Jewish, therefore illegal, and she was living under a false name. "Charlotte Maly, neé Kramereit" was what it said in her identity papers. She was worried about being discovered and wanted to get new documents and find an inconspicuous way to travel to Munich from Berlin.

Who was this woman? Andrea Wolffenstein was the daughter of a city building contractor, and her parents and Donata's had known each other for years. Donata remembered their childhood – as a three or four-year old she had admired Andrea who was already seven or eight years old then. Sometimes she was kind and played with me, and on top of everything she would let me play with her little dog "Flocki." You don't forget such special treatment! Suddenly the old memories came alive again – the childhood games, the walks that they took as young girls in the Weimar park, the excursions into the Thuringian woods or the nearby Schloss Belvedere. Later they met only sporadically, even though they were both living in Berlin. Finally they lost touch with each other. Their lives were too different – one had devoted herself to her family and numerous activities, the other, to her career as a pianist.

Now they were sitting across from each other in the living room on Westend Allee, catching up on their lives and looking for a way to help Andrea in the immediate future.

Donata might have invented the saying "'Geht nicht' gibt's nicht" ("There's no such thing as 'it can't be done.'") And of course this time too she didn't get discouraged just because the task was a difficult one. As so often before she thought up a little scenario and took various "steps." It goes without saying that Andrea would have a bed and a roof over her head at our house for the run of the "performance."

After taking a look at Andrea's identification card, Donata thought that, although it wasn't very convincing, she should keep the name "Maly"; otherwise it would unnecessarily complicate matters. Then she went to the police with a pretended display of annoyance. She said a Mrs. Maly from Drohobycz had turned up at her home, a secretary of her husband's, and in the general chaos accompanying the military retreat, the stupid woman had unfortunately lost her identification card. But luckily she still had the notice of her departure from Drohobycz (they had of course forged that). "I don't like having to put up a stranger in my house; after all, I'm not running a pension!" she said indignantly. What could be done about this?

"The first thing is for the woman to get food ration coupons," the officer said pleasantly. "Then you'll at least not have to worry about that." And he promised to get her a substitute identity card as soon as possible.

And she actually received a certificate for the desired "cards." She went immediately to the place of issue and was handed all the blessed documents: food ration card, clothing card, and even smoker's stamps. That certainly was a start!

The next act of the drama dealt with finding a means of travel for Andrea. She had found out that you couldn't take the fast express train anymore without permission, and she had been advised to use only the slow passenger trains and to change trains several times during the trip. Donata immediately dismissed this plan as much too dangerous. "It would be highly conspicuous for you to be getting off at some little shitty station and then getting on the next train. No, you'd have to be crazy to do that!" I'm sure she was right. But how was one to get permission for the express train? One would have to go to the police again and not only give them a very convincing reason but also be able to show proof.

"I know how we'll accomplish it," Donata decided. She took a blank piece of paper and put it into her typewriter. At the top left she typed the name: "Dr. Meta Mühlenkamp" and at the top right she typed a Tübingen address. Both were total inventions.

"Dear Mrs. Maly," Dr. Meta Mühlenkamp wrote, "I liked your application very much. I would be happy for you to start in the position at my office as soon as possible. I find that taking care of my practice, the household, and the children all by myself is too great a strain for me for any length of time. It is more than I can manage. I hope these lines will be sufficient for you to obtain permission to use the express train. However, should you not be able to get the permission from the appropriate Berlin office, then I'll simply have to wait until the employment office in Tübingen will confirm the necessity of this. - Looking forward to working with you, Heil Hitler!"

(signed) Dr. Meta Mühlenkamp."

Armed with this letter, which she'd wrinkled a little so that it wouldn't look too new, she again went to the appropriate office

Very sweetly and acting helpless, she took out the letter and asked the gentlemen if it would be sufficient. The man in charge shook his head with misgiving – he felt the letter was not enough.

"Oh, how annoying," Donata sighed. "I'm stuck with this stranger, and obviously she can't find a decent job – and look, this doctor probably has a very good reason for writing with such urgency." And she went on with a worried expression, "Oh, well, if you are not authorized to issue this form, then she'll have no other recourse than to sit on the local train for days, or wait until she hears from the employment office in Tübingen. I hope Mrs. Maly's job won't be gone by then."

Hard to know whether the official felt honor-bound or whether he was sorry for the poor woman standing so downcast before him. In any event he changed his tune. "Well, perhaps there would be a lot of waste involved here. You know what? I'll give you the travel permission now, then the woman can take the train, and you'll finally be rid of her."

My mother thanked him and, her face beaming, handed Andrea the document. She also duly reported that "Mrs. Maly" had left the city. "Next place of residence: Tübingen," is what it says on the copy she had them make at the Berlin Reparations Office. Andrea, her old friend, could now continue her travels southward.

After the detour to Tübingen she finally arrived in Munich. There, she and her sister supported themselves by making golden leaf clusters for officers' uniforms at home.

They kept in touch with my mother after the war, if rather sporadically. In a letter Andrea wrote, dated September 10, 1985, that I found in a file after my mother's death, it says: "Your phone call reminds me to tell you how very gratefully Vally and

I think of you. People who didn't live through those times can't possibly imagine the risk your incredibly brave actions posed to you. You helped us, together with others, to more than forty years of happy sisterly togetherness. After all this time, I wanted at last to tell you this."

34

Immediately after the July 20, 1944 attempt on Adolf Hitler's life, the city was full of rumors: The assassination attempt was successful and Hitler is dead; the attempt failed, and Hitler is alive; Hitler is dead but the Nazi leadership wants to make people think that nothing happened to him. But it wouldn't be until Hitler addresses the people on the radio that the failure of the attack would be a certainty. For days no names are named; they only talk about a "small clique of traitors." Every day there is new speculation about who was involved, whom they've arrested.

Heinrich Himmler, who has been informed of the findings in the investigations, immediately put into effect a large-scale arrest operation. Terror reigned. House searches, interrogations, torture became everyday occurrences; the relatives and families of the conspirators were held liable for their crimes.

The anxious question in every family, in all the circles of those who had opposed Hitler was: Were any of our friends among them, anyone we know? In the weeks after the assassination attempt it would turn out that there were some among the Helmriches' acquaintances who were affected. Not any of the so-called main conspirators who were put to death on the gallows at Plötzensee Prison, but people from the military and civilian circles who were in the opposition. They were all in prison on Lehrter Strasse.

Donata promised to check, as much as she could, both on those she knew and those she didn't know, for after all she lived in the same city, and Westend Allee wasn't all that far from the prison. She submitted a petition and was given permission to bring food for the prisoners. For months my mother and my two sisters took turns twice a week to make the difficult trip to the Lehrter Strasse prison, always accompanied by the fear that something might have happened to one of their protégées. They walked through the debris and ruins, past the Lehrter Bahnhof riddled with bullets, in constant fear that public traffic would be halted again or that they'd be surprised by an air raid alarm before they got back home. Such a disaster was an ever-present threat during that last year of the war. It was forbidden and a punishable offense to stay out on the street during an alarm; one had to go at once into the nearest air-raid shelter. Those living in the inner city had little faith in the safety of these places – they were to be avoided whenever possible. Fear of coming home and not finding your own home there anymore was an ever-present concern on each return trip.

My older sister remembers the depressing atmosphere surrounding the prison. She says there were long lines of people waiting in front of a large gate, almost all of them, women. After the gate was opened with a tremendous creaking and rattling, a certain number of those waiting were allowed to go in, and the gate was closed again behind them with the same terrible creaking and rattling. The women inside then formed a new line in front of a small counter. The closer they got to their goal, the uneasier they felt.

At that fateful counter they handed over the food, cigarettes, soap, and clean laundry, sometimes even little scraps of paper concealed in a loaf of bread. They took dirty clothes back home to be washed. For hours on end the women waited anxiously. From the perspective of decency and morality, they were a German elite. At each visit they were afraid of finding out that the one for whom they had brought things wasn't there anymore. "These things won't be needed anymore. You can take them back with you," they would be told. My older sister tells about women who collapsed and about the others standing around them trying to console them in a hopeless situation. This heavy blow could strike any one of them the next time.

The younger of my sisters recalls that during her first "excursion" to Lehrter Strasse she shyly gave the hated "Heil Hitler" salute. One of the ladies waiting there said, "Child, you don't have to say that here – they already know how we feel."

It was shortly before Christmas, and those who were waiting were talking about what the holiday might bring. The younger of my sisters, who had in the meantime gotten back her confident rebelliousness, turned to a young SS man who was one of the guards and said, "And what's your wish for Christmas?"

"I'm wishing for bread coupons," he answered simply.

Her surprise couldn't have been greater. "You? You of all people wish for bread coupons?" my sister asked nonplussed.

"Yes, because there are prisoners here who don't get any visitors," the young man said to her. Once the war was over, he was put on trial at which it was revealed that in 1944, at the age of eighteen, he was not entirely voluntarily drafted into the Waffen SS and that as a guard in a prison had done everything he could to help the prisoners. After the testimony of witnesses, he was released.

"My poor daughter," Donata said later with regret. "The younger one wasn't even eighteen yet – but I told the girl that it had to be done, and with that the matter was closed."

It was not unusual to give bribes in the hope that it would improve the lot of the prisoners. This was the case not only at the entry gate to the Lehrter Strasse prison. Several books, on the subject, give an insight into the often bewildering and muddled structures of this kind of "additional help." Honest opponents of the regime, Party members who played a double game, and swindlers and con-men were all part of such networks. Donata could remember a mysterious incident, whose beginning and end always remained a puzzle for her.

One day someone she knew from Berlin-Lichtenrade turned to her. He wasn't one of the innermost circle, but rather one on the periphery of the conspiratorial community. Yet apparently he trusted my mother's organizational talent, and she had no doubt about the urgency of his request. It was a matter of rounding up as quickly as possible, four thousand cigarettes for a special purpose. It sounded crazy. But Donata didn't ask for what or for whom this considerable number of cigarettes was needed — and she never did find out. The time-honored rule was: The less you know, the less they can get out of you by torture.

She lost no time in getting to work. A genius in making and keeping up useful contacts, she went to see Josef at the warehouse. He was a Belgian-Flemish worker who had put our garden back into shape after the unfortunate big bunker affair; my mother had invited him to our Christmas Eve celebration the previous year, 1943. Now she asked him, coming straight to the point, whether he would be able in a very short time to obtain four thousand cigarettes – she could offer him a considerable number of bread coupons and also some cash in exchange.

"All right, *Mamitje*, it will be done!" he said, and the next day the cigarettes were already in Donata's hands. By some roundabout way that no one quite remembers any more, they were then smuggled into the prison, and there they seemed to have fulfilled their purpose. She could never find out any more.

Immediately after July 20th, Hermann Göring, as the highest-ranking officer of the Wehrmacht, issued a decree that today seems merely a ridiculous anecdote. Back then it was no less than a break with a long military tradition. All the units of the Army were advised to use only the "Hitler Salute" in greeting one another. From now on, instead of placing their hands up to their caps in a gesture of salute, all German soldiers had to raise their arms in the Hitler greeting. This was more than a symbol – it was a visible gesture of submission. That's how it was intended, and that's how it was understood and in spite of that, or maybe precisely for that reason, it was complied with.

35

I remember that the last months of the war were a sort of in-between stage for me, a time that was stuck between other times. Of course in the country, in the village of Müggenburg, life went on normally following the seasons. The potatoes were put into the storage pit, the apples on the fruit racks, the cattle stayed in the barn, and for Christmas, as always, we had a Christmas goose. And still, everything was different. A palpable tension hung over our daily lives, and even we children sensed that big things were about to happen, even here on our peaceful peninsula.

The grown-ups spoke freely about the advance of the Americans, English, and French forces in the West and the Red Army in the East. Mention of Hitler's "miracle weapon" was greeted with laughter – nobody there seemed to believe in it. People listened eagerly and quite overtly to the BBC's German-language broadcasts; because of them, I had a pretty good picture of what was happening – as much as was possible for a nine- or ten-year-old.

In the fall of 1944 my father, whom I had missed so very much, came for a very short but long anticipated visit. I was overjoyed! What I didn't know back them was that his visit wasn't just to see me, but also to see Tosia, a young Polish woman. Her real name was Sylvia and she was Jewish and in hiding. She had been brought from Drohobycz to Berlin to my mother, and from there she went to Müggenburg to stay with Uncle Friedel and Aunt Maria.

We all longed for the war to end. I had my own very personal reason – I wanted at last to be reunited with my mother, father, siblings, and Hedda. Besides, I felt as if I'd been ostracized. Sure,

I was well nourished, but I was very sad. Only later did I realize how important it had been for my mother to know that her child was well fed and safe. But children who have never known real hunger, have no understanding for such things. I felt sorry for myself and bitterly alone. That was ungrateful of me, and many people told me as much; besides, it wasn't even true.

Every day at dinner, the talk centered on our hopes and wishes that this crazy time might soon come to an end. But there was also increasingly explicit anxiety expressed about what was in store for us then. It wasn't only the fear that this area on the Baltic Sea might suddenly turn into a conflict area – there was a growing dread of the Russians. They had a reputation of being unpredictable, and those who knew the havoc the Germans had wrought in the East, were afraid of retaliation. It's also possible that Hitler's propaganda contributed to the deep feeling of unease among the people. I remember clearly that even the Polish women, Sophie and Marianne, as well as Anna from the Ukraine who helped our Aunt Hilde with the housekeeping, were not looking forward with unalloyed joy to their liberation by the Russian Army. They had no idea what their immediate future would hold for them and were worried about it.

In the fall of 1944, Uncle Friedel decided that we all had to learn Russian since we'd be conquered by the Russians pretty soon. And we did. He had found a book, it was called *1000 Words of Russian* and had been published as part of a popular series of language guides for different languages, all called *1000 Words of…*. After that, we would sit in a conspiratorial circle in front of the living room fireplace in the evenings and try to learn at least some snatches of that difficult language. I recall thinking it was a lot of fun.

After the Russians marched in, our meager knowledge of the language did indeed prove useful. Months later it was great to see the amazement of young Cossacks when I spoke to them in Russian.

Of course there was no doubt that our enemy, Mr. Muëller, would not have understood our language studies at all. He certainly wouldn't have reacted well to our eagerness to learn if he had known what words we were cramming. For even so close to the end of their reign, the men in brown and black showed no weakness and knew no mercy – only a very few of them allowed themselves even a partial realization of what was happening.

A beautiful spring was spreading its glory all around us even as we began hearing the growling of the "Stalin organs" in the distance. Then, as they came closer and closer, the far-away growl turned into loud thunder. The forsythia bloomed in March; in April the horse chestnut trees burst into bloom, and we put on our summery clothes. But our rural independence, being able to roam through the countryside, play in the horses' paddock and in the woods was over. We children were now given strict orders to stay within earshot of the house.

Then came the day when we were supposed to put on as many layers of clothes as we could – in spite of its being very warm – hurry, hurry! All women and children were being taken to Kirr Island. We were rowed across in two rowboats. We children were very excited. We slept in one room, on the floor, and I remember that, rather than being afraid, I thought it all a thrilling adventure.

I think it was probably only two days later when we saw our first Russian liberator – he was slowly opening the door to our room, and he had Aunt Maria's accordion casually slung over his shoulder. The instrument was emitting some miserable notes, and the soldier had a funny expression on his face. No sooner would his eyes rest on one of us, than he would avert his gaze. It turned out he was completely sloshed! The adults couldn't agree what to make of this – was it a good sign or a bad sign.

Soon after this encounter we found out by word of mouth that as the Russians were advancing, shortly before they arrived on the Darss Penninsula, they had seized a ship intended for the SS with four thousand bottles of Schnapps on board.

The few Russians we caught sight of on Kirr moved off again the following day. I can't remember anything happening to any of the women. In those days "rape" certainly was no longer a foreign word for me. I knew pretty well that all the women were afraid of having it happen to them. Aunt Maria, people whispered, was grabbed by a drunk Russian, but before he could really "get down to business" she got away from him by jumping out of the window. The soldiers rummaged around in their pants pockets for sticky candies and gave them to us children. "Don't refuse anything! Or they'll get angry," we were told. As if we would have turned down anything as rare as a sugary candy!

While we were safely stowed away on Kirr waiting to see what would happen next, Uncle Friedel with one or two other men, all carrying white flags, had gone to meet the Russians. A first acid test for our Russian lessons.

A couple of days later, when the war was finally over, we all returned to the village. With feelings of sadness, I held on to first Sophie's, then Marianne's hand when we had to say goodbye and farewell, for I sensed that we would never see one another again. During that goodbye I wished for nothing so much as that I would also be able to go home again, to Berlin. However, my mother, Aunt Maria, and Uncle Friedel decided it would be best for me if I stayed on in Müggenburg for the time being. And so I had to wait until August 1946, the beginning of the new school year, before I could finally return home. At least my oldest sister came to visit me for two weeks. She played some of the old, familiar pieces on the piano, and went swimming with me.

Now, a new period was starting in our village. The "Russian period" and postwar life in the SBZ, the Soviet Occupation Zone. Now the farm workers were no longer Poles and Ukrainians, but Germans fleeing from the East. They liked to threaten us with the *Occupation* and the *Kommandatura*, sometimes used by the Russians to discipline the defeated people, sometimes by the Germans who wanted to defend themselves against attacks by the soldiers.

There was also something joyful and unexpected that happened during that long, sunny summer of 1945 – the Cossacks came with their adorable little horses, which they let us children ride. Things were still topsy-turvy on the Darss, so the adults couldn't spend much time with us children, and we had more freedom than we had ever known before. We learned Russian commands like, "Woman, come here" and incorporated it into our games. The words *Uri, Uri* meant hand over your watches, and we all knew that our bicycles were in constant danger of being stolen by the Russians and being ridden till they were wrecked. Once I was riding Aunt Maria's big bicycle on the village street, standing up on the pedals because the seat was much too high for me, when two Russian soldiers came toward me and pointed at the bicycle. In my panic I got off and ran away as fast as I could, pushing the bicycle. I obviously had more faith in my legs than in the much-too-big bicycle! When I cautiously turned around, I saw that the two soldiers had stopped and were doubled over with laughter.

Our everyday lives didn't settle down until the fall of 1945. Our time of unfettered freedom was at an end. The Cossacks left; a new regiment – without horses – came to the Darss, and in late September classes started again in the small village school. If I'm right, it wasn't long after this that the first blue shirts of the Free German Youth (*Freie Deutsche Jugend*), "FDJ" for short, turned up. I remember clearly that Rudi – an older neighbor boy who had been one of the few boys in the village who had worn the brown shirt with the leather knot under the chin of the Hitler Youth – proudly showed us his new blue shirt one day.

36

At the beginning of 1945, more and more people started leaving the German capital and fleeing westward on terribly overcrowded trains. They were afraid of being conquered by the Russians and so they tried to escape to another place. In the eyes of the Nazis who never tired of pushing their propaganda about the final victory, this was probably punishable defeatism – but who could have stopped all those people?

In February or March of that year the younger of my sisters said goodbye to us. She was eighteen and said that her fear of the Russians made staying in Berlin impossible for her. Today she thinks that it was only partly responsible for her desire to leave. Actually, she simply wanted to have more freedom – to get away from her over-protective mother whose care she found too restrictive. She went to Hamburg where she found a room to sublet and dreamed about a career as an actress. She was probably in touch with Eberhard Helmrich, but she of all my siblings was the one who was least close to him. She wanted to lead her own life and go her own way.

During those weeks when the end of the "Thousand-year Reich" seemed close enough to touch, there were again rumors that the leadership would no longer spare the "privileged" among the Jews. They were to be separated from their "Aryan" wives or husbands and taken away, the rumors had it. There was actually an order dated January 15, 1945, to deport the affected Jews in mass transports to Theresienstadt by February 15th. The cities lay in ruins, the roads were jammed with hordes of refugees, the Wehrmacht was in retreat on all fronts – and in spite of that such transports were still being organized in most of the large cities toward the end of the second week in February! However, only some of the deportations actually took place. The capacity for such actions just didn't exist anymore, and the general chaos of the war was more than even the most dedicated proponents of the "Final Solution" could cope with. Nevertheless, they managed to ship the unfortunate people who were in the Berlin Jewish Hospital to the Brandenburg Concentration Camps Sachsenhausen and Ravensbrück. These were the last deportations.

The Allied air raids did not let up during those weeks and months. Now there were also frequent daytime air raid alarms, in addition to the nighttime ones. Electricity, gas, and water as well as telephone service kept being interrupted, sometimes for hours, sometimes even for days at a time. All normal communication had gone to blazes. The residents of the capital were living in a rumor society; they picked up and spread all sorts of rumors. They no longer knew what the other parts of the city looked like, information was reliable only as far as the next street corner.

Meanwhile the front was moving ever closer. "Weren't you terribly afraid?" I asked my mother a few years later. She thought about it briefly and then slowly shook her head. "No, strange to say, not at all!" When everything around you is lost, maybe then you also lose your fear, who knows.

Not that Donata was carefree or careless, certainly not. But she probably needed all her energy to go on living and to put one foot in front of the other, to cope with the next thing. It wasn't her way to sink into paralyzing apathy.

The three women – Donata, her oldest daughter, and of course Hedda – held the fort in the familiar house on Westend Allee. They had been very lucky, for except for a few broken windowpanes and other more minor damage, the house had so far remained untouched. My mother and the remaining sister had always had an especially close relationship, but during that time it turned into a tight, enduring bond. "We weren't just mother and daughter," Donata said later. "We were also something like war comrades. We went together to extinguish the fires, we dragged furniture out of burning houses and into the street – we really did everything together."

There was something else they shared too, and that was a special kind of concern and responsibility. During that period they were hiding a guest in an attic room, an old persecuted Jewish woman whose health worried them. A doctor friend on Mother's list, who had already helped many illegal people, did what he could for her, but it wasn't enough, not the kind of medical care that would have been available under normal conditions. My mother and sister tried to figure out what they would do if the woman were to die. They finally decided that there was only one way to handle it – at night during an air raid alarm, when it was to be hoped no one else would be outside, they would place the poor woman on a street some few yards away from the house. Luckily it never came to that. The woman recovered somewhat, went into hiding elsewhere, and lived to experience the liberation.

For many Berlin men and women the conquest of their city began when they suddenly realized that the daily, ear-splitting crashing and splintering was no longer being caused by bombs being dropped from planes, but by artillery guns. The Russians had arrived! They were here! The battle for the German Reich's capital had begun. It was waged doggedly, and was extraordinarily bloody. It lasted seventeen long days and nights. In contrast to the cities occupied quickly and without much bloodshed by the Western Allies – people spoke jokingly of "capitulation by telephone" – Berlin was defended in senseless house-to-house and street-by-street battles, and therefore subjected to even worse destruction. As late as May 2, 1945, Grand Admiral Dönitz directed the following mendacious order of the day to the Wehrmacht:

"To the German Army! My Comrades! The Führer is

dead. Abiding by his great idea to save the people of Europe from Bolshevism, he sacrificed his life and met with a hero's death. With his death one of the greatest heroes of German history has passed away. We lower our flags in proud reverence and loyalty. The Führer has appointed me to succeed him as Head of State, and Supreme Leader of the Wehrmacht. I assume the high command over all sections of the German Wehrmacht with the determination to continue the fight against Bolshevism as long as it takes to save the fighting forces and the thousands of families of the German Eastern territories from slavery and annihilation. I must continue the fight against the British and the Americans as far and as long as they continue to hinder me in fighting the Bolshevists. The situation demands continued and unconditional commitment from you who have already accomplished such historically great deeds and are longing for the end of the War. I demand discipline and obedience. Only by carrying out my orders without reservation will chaos and our defeat be avoided. Anyone who does not fulfill his duty, thereby bringing death and enslavement to German women and children, is a coward and a traitor. The oath of loyalty you have each of you sworn to the Führer now applies to me as the Führer's chosen successor. German men, do your duty, the life of our people depends on it!"

The pathetic suicide of the "Führer" was sold as a "hero's death" while men who didn't want to follow the Führer's orders anymore were shot or hanged.

Donata and the people living in the immediate neighborhood watched in horror as the Red Army set up their guns on the other side of a train embankment about two hundred yards behind the houses on Westend Allee. It took only a short time until the SS turned up and ordered all the houses to be evacuated, because this was to be the place where a defensive rampart was to be built. So now, at the very end, our family and our neighbors were in the line of fire and had to find some other place to take shelter. Farewell, dear Westend Allee!

All the residents had to leave their houses, and my mother, sister and Hedda found shelter nearby in the cellar of the Church of the Holy Ghost (*Heilig-Geist Kirche*) with the Steyler Missionaries. There were about fifty people camping in this not very large room. The three women had pretty much lost any sense of time, which is why their recollection of how long they stayed there is only vague. Perhaps three days, but maybe it was as long as five or six. Still, my sister clearly remembers that the Padres handed out soup. The beneficent and apparently unshakable calm these pious men radiated provided a sharp contrast to the general disorganization all around them, and the strain people were under. It reassured them.

Occasionally it was possible to use the telephone. Men and women from other districts of Berlin who were stranded here, desperately tried to reach their relatives. The Russians had supposedly already occupied the nearby Eichkamp locality, and horrendous rumors were spreading.

Donata became increasingly nervous – the crowding, the lack of space, and all the rumors and stories affected her. She racked her mind about how and when they could get out of the church cellar, and decided to return home as quickly as possible, in spite of the hospitality of the Padres. She thought it would be better to take shelter in their own bunker in the back corner of the garden.

So the little group set out, and when they reached Westend Allee, they were relieved to see no evidence at all of any defensive rampart and all their houses standing there just as they had left them.

My mother, sister, and Hedda went into the bunker; a woman

from the neighborhood joined them, and so they waited. They must have imagined dozens of times during the previous months what it would be like once the war was over. An explosion of joy, jubilant relief, and thankfulness! The reality was quite different.

The women settled down in their circular bunker den and had deep conversations about Goethe and Schiller. My sister swears to it. Suddenly they heard steps on the stairs. A man peered in through the door opening that was protected by a mattress and said simply: "The war is finished!" Then he went away. The women looked at each other dumbstruck, didn't move. Something had to happen now, they thought. But nothing at all happened.

After Donata had recovered from the shock – she was probably the first to do so – she said, "Well, now that the war's over, we can go back inside our house." They all got up, climbed up the stairs and cautiously looked around; then they took the path through the garden and into the house. Once inside, Hedda cooked them all some pea soup – her first post-war act – and all the women sat down around the table and calmly enjoyed their first meal without the fear of sirens and bombs.

Even though the National Socialists had capitulated, there was to be one last, tragic and totally senseless war victim in our immediate neighborhood. A good and reliable friend of ours through all those difficult years was suddenly confronted by two young SS people who had forced their way into his house and were gesturing excitedly with their weapons.

"The war is over; put away your weapons!" the man said to the two, but they refused. Then he suggested that if they didn't want to turn the guns in at the officially designated place, they could hand them over to him.

"What right do you have to tell us what to do?" they said belligerently.

"You are in my home!"

Thereupon they shot the man. His wife, who was in the

adjoining room, heard it all.

Even in the midst of the worst chaos, Donata remained true to her convictions. When the Russians left their gun emplacements and came walking through the garden and toward the house, she followed Eberhard's urgent advice: "Don't ever lock anything!" She left the door open and greeted the soldiers. She offered them tea and showed them where they could wash. She retained her talent for hospitality even in this new, unpredictable situation. She didn't think that people would kill – or rape – someone after they've eaten or had something to drink together. My sister, of course, had stayed out of sight and gone up to the attic. Luckily one of the soldiers, an officer, spoke French fairly fluently, so that they could all converse with one another.

Admittedly, the three women were incredibly lucky that nothing happened to them.

They weren't even robbed. Except for an old-fashioned portable phonograph and a few shellac records, everything remained where it was. In other areas of Berlin conditions were much worse. We knew about this from the many reports we'd heard. Not until the British, Americans, and French arrived two months later and Berlin was divided into four sectors, did life return to being more than merely a a matter of surviving. During that time, many of those who had fled to the West returned and were appalled to find their belongings and property not as they had left them. One woman neighbor, finding her sewing machine gone, reproached Donata for not having taken better care of it.

Donata just said, "I suggest that during the next war you stay here and take care of your things yourself!"

There's one other bizarre incident I'd like to mention that occurred during those days in early May – this one, too, was typical for Donata who remained true to her principles and at the same time quite unpredictable, inconsistent, and generous. A very young SS man came to the house with a small cart. Suddenly he was standing at the front door. He asked her for some civilian clothes. My mother recognized him as one of the guards from the prison on Lehrter Strasse. He had always behaved decently toward the prisoners and their visitors. So she gave him one of her husband's gray jackets. He thanked her and left. She did it, so to speak, in violation of her own vow back then never to help any of that lot. "But," she added apologetically, "there are situations where in spite of everything, you can find a reason to give one of them a jacket."

37

The city I returned to as an eleven-year-old in August 1946 was a heap of rubble. In spite of that it seemed exciting and alive to me. Berlin had a lot to offer – the theater, concerts, and the movies. And finally books reappeared, the books Hitler had prevented his people from reading. The grown-ups in my neighborhood greedily and enthusiastically absorbed what they could of the cultural developments that had taken place in the meantime outside Germany. And the lights were on again everywhere, unless there happened to be an interruption in the electrical service. The time of the depressing "blackouts and brown-outs" was a distant past we had overcome.

Berlin had turned into a multilingual city; it had a multicultural population; back then we didn't yet know this word for it. The soldiers of the occupation armies and their families, foreigners from many nations, refugees, and thousands of Jewish DPs (Displaced Persons) from Eastern Europe who were waiting to emigrate abroad or to Palestine lived in the city. The passengers riding the S-Bahn were also a polyglot lot. My mother and I had a sort of game between us, trying to translate what we overheard into German. She was the "expert" in English and French with a few phrases from other western languages thrown in; I reciprocated by softly translating Russian conversations into German.

The people of Berlin were more or less adapting to living with their former enemies and victims. Whether they were "Ami sweethearts," nursemaids working for young parents from the DP camps, or "housekeepers" for English officers' families – all these relationships had one pragmatic principle in common: service in exchange for goods that you couldn't buy in any German

Donata Helmrich, 1945 in Berlin

shop. This worked for both sides. The immediate past remained irrelevant during that period of transition. It could only have interfered. We were living not just in a time of transition, but also in a society in transition.

After the years at the little Müggenburg village school, I now went to a modern-language high school for girls, the Westend School that my two older sisters had attended. The old school building, however, wasn't available for classes because it was being used as a hospital. And so we were taught in two other

Donata Helmrich, 1947 in Berlin

buildings. The lower grades were housed in the Leistikow School, my old grammar school; the upper grades, ten minutes away, in a large vacant Villa on Bayern Allee, where only a little while earlier the "Armaments Command of the Wehrmacht" had presided. The teachers had to walk back and forth from the one school to the other between classes, which gave us additional break time.

Westend students weren't the only ones who used these rooms. We shared them with students of the Herder School, a high school for boys, which didn't have a school building of its own either. As was customary in many of the city's schools back then, we were taught in shifts: One week we had classes in the morning, the next week in the afternoon. That really worked quite well, and I don't remember any occasions when we had no classes, except when it was extremely cold, with temperatures far below freezing. Of course we tried to find out the names of the boys who sat in our seats – and the other way around – and we wrote each other little notes that we left in the inkwells in our desks.

At that time there were many women without husbands, and many children without fathers. They had died in the war or were prisoners of war. The Helmrich family, at least its Berlin contingent, continued to be made up of our mother, my oldest sister, Hedda, and me. My brother didn't come back from his Russian prisoner-of-war captivity until November 1947. The younger of my two sisters had decided to stay in Hamburg for the time being. She had found an interesting job there with the Nordwestdeutsche Rundfunk (Northwest German Broadcasting).

And our father? He was still alive, and living in Germany only a few hours' train ride away from us. Why didn't he come back to us? I was terribly disappointed when my mother told me point-blank that this was not possible. After all, she added, I knew that he was a farmer, and at the moment there was no work for him in Berlin. And so he had to stay in West Germany.

Did I really believe her explanation? I know only that I didn't ask again after that. Today I wonder why I was satisfied with her answer. Was I afraid of the truth? Did I have any idea that there might have been other reasons for his staying away?

Soon after the war my mother began to work as a translator and foreign-language secretary for an American News Agency in the Zehlendorf District. The advantages of her job there were impressive: Besides her salary, she got genuine hot coffee daily and a hot lunch in the canteen. And she had a heated place to work. Nevertheless there was one very strict rule for my mother

School teacher Hildegard Kranold, 1953

as well as for all other German employees, and it was a hard one to obey: Any leftover food had to go into the garbage! Large amounts of it met that fate. It was forbidden to take any back home, at the risk of being fired. This sort of waste in hungry Berlin had its reasons: They wanted to avoid the temptation to sell anything on the black market. Whether it really worked is doubtful. My mother often worked until late at night; and would be brought home in an open Jeep. That really impressed me. Who else had a mother who drove in a Jeep! But she herself found it less delightful as the weather got colder and colder. She would get home frozen through and through with no way to warm up, for our house, like most of the houses in Berlin, was not heated. There was no coal, at any rate no affordable coal.

Cornelia Helmrich (left), after her graduation, 1954

Unfortunately, Mother's first attempt to develop a source of income fell through. Neuwestend was in the British Sector, and so she had the idea to collect all the English-language books from all the bookshelves scattered throughout our house. She found some three hundred. Crime stories, novels, children's books – a big haul. She furnished one of the rooms on the ground floor as a modest lending library and waited eagerly for customers. But tough luck and bad timing. Two weeks after she opened her little library, the British Military Administration opened their own library not far from our house. And they had three thousand volumes! A little sign on the outside of our house, "The English Library," remained there for some time, testimony to mother's unlucky beginning as an independent entrepreneur.

My sister had also found work: Every afternoon she went to the newly set-up YMCA on the Reichsstrasse and gave English soldiers piano lessons. Here too there were "fringe benefits" even more attractive than the money she earned. Of course the rooms were heated, and at tea time there was real tea and two pieces of cake. And she shared this delicacy with her youngest sister. She ate one piece and brought the other piece back home for me in a little tin box. They didn't object to this at the YMCA. I assure you that no cake in the world ever tasted so good.

Our dear Miss Hedda stayed on with us, taking care of the household, of me, and of our cats. She could of course have found work with a family of the Allied forces, but she didn't. She stayed loyal to us, determined to share the good times with our family as well as the bad.

The Helmriches' lot was no different from that of all the other Berliners – you lived frugally and tried to get a little bit extra on top of the usual rations to have enough to eat. We stayed away from the Black Market profiteers who traded just about anything, demanding horrendous prices. But I remember a woman whom we'd baptized *Taschentantchen* (Bag Auntie) because she appeared at our door now and then loaded down with bags. Sometimes she had butter, sometimes eggs, and sometimes even "genuine" coffee, rare delicacies that mother bought from her or bartered in exchange for any valuables she still had left.

In those days there was a girl in my class who was obviously better dressed than the rest of us and who always had fabulous sandwiches to eat during recess. I asked my mother how come, and whether the girl was maybe a "profiteer's child."

"No," she said, "those people are OdF, and for a change they're doing really well now."

OdF stood for *Opfer des Faschismus*, Victims of Fascism, and that meant they received special rations among other things.

"And what about us?" I asked her.

"Us? Come on now we weren't persecuted!" And that explained it all. But whether I was completely in agreement with that view of things I can't say for sure. In any case, the enticing fantasies about the future I had during the Nazi times crumbled pretty quickly. The rewarding of the good people and the punishment of the bad didn't work out as well in the real world as it did in the fairytales.

For a long time after the war, the subject of National Socialism was considered taboo in the schools as well as in offices and within families. It was never mentioned, not among the students nor in the classroom. For that reason it was undreamt of for our German language and history teacher, the wonderful, unforgettable Hildegard Kranold, to include this subject in our lessons. It must have been in 1951 when she, so to speak, came clean about the nuts and bolts of the Third Reich. With her we read "Moabit Sonnets" written by Albrecht Haushofer, who was executed in April 1945, and "Last Letters from Tegel Prison" by Helmut James Graf von Moltke, who was executed as well. She also introduced us to the life and thoughts of Dietrich Bonhoeffer and Helmut Gollwitzer.

I remember that her independent decision to introduce the subject resulted in angry protests from many parents, and that there were some students who refused to confront the truth about that period. But apparently none of this disturbed our "Kranold," for she continued to deal in her classes with this highly sensitive subject, which was generally kept under wraps, or treated as if it never happened. The fact that the school principal didn't muzzle her speaks well for him.

Many years would pass before the Nazi period would be included in the lesson plans of schools. Not until the end of the sixties did they expect students – or rather their parents – to overcome the inertia of memory and to lift the taboo.

At home on Westend Allee we wondered during those years

what had become of the various former victims we had helped, and where they were now. Not all of them got in touch with mother after the war. In some cases, she was really disappointed. But on the other hand, it wasn't surprising. Persons trying to leave a depressing past behind them won't turn around to look back. They are more likely to look to the future. Some however, did get in touch. They wrote letters or sent CARE packages from America that we longed for eagerly and received gratefully. We got to know about corned beef, dried eggs, ham in raisin sauce, and other astonishing and unfamiliar things that came in cans. These packages were not delivered to our home, but the addressee received a postcard with the information that a package was ready to be picked up. Good Lord in Heaven, what joy there was at our house whenever one of those cards dropped through the mail slot!

Meanwhile, the Helmriches didn't spend too much time looking back either. Mother observed the people around her very carefully. She still rigorously divided her fellow citizens into "Nazis" and "Not Nazis" and watched, not without bitterness, as they came creeping out of their holes and got on with their lives without being challenged about their earlier behavior. She retained her strict standards about whom you could be good friends with and whom you'd better keep your distance from. A person you could unhesitatingly entrust with your own children in times of need and persecution was "all right." For a time she even made the exorbitant claim that she could recognize a Nazi by the nape of his neck.

38

The months went by and my father didn't come home. Not even for a visit. Of course, traveling wasn't easy in those days – but still, he could at least have shown up once! I assume that we wrote letters to each other back then, but I don't remember anymore what they said. It was probably a pretty boring exchange because neither he nor I managed to tell each other what really concerned us.

Eberhard had, in the meantime, found a minor job with the Food and Nutrition Office in Hamburg. He moved to Frankfurt in 1947 where he worked for an agency charged with managing agriculture in the Western Zones. During that time he must have come to the decision that he no longer wanted to live in Germany.

He had believed in a new beginning, and hoped that the specters of the recent past had been driven out. He was mistaken – the many who were still left were everywhere, sitting in their starting holes, working in government offices and industry. Diligently they covered up everything they didn't want to know about. And so he decided to leave his homeland and began the process of emigrating.

At the time I had no inkling of his plans.

In the fall of 1948, during the blockade, he came one last time to Berlin. My oldest sister was away for a few months enjoying the hospitality of old friends of my parents in the south of England, and my mother had gone there too for a short visit. She was still there when my father arrived. She had planned to fly back in time to see him, but she was stuck in London, just as he was stuck in Berlin. There was heavy fog that did not lift for many days. All of Berlin wondered when the planes could fly again. At that time, during the Berlin Blockade, no other means of transportation

Eberhard Helmrich, November 1948
| Foto Hofmann, Frankfurt am Main

was possible; the only way in or out was by plane. The city was dependent on air traffic.

Meanwhile, I realized that something wasn't quite right between my parents. But since they didn't talk about very private matters, certainly not "with the child," I felt pretty alone with my fears. Along with the joy of finally seeing my father again, I was afraid that my parents might miss seeing each other. Obviously I was under the illusion that everything would turn out all right again if only my parents could meet and talk to each other. Maybe, I thought, we might have to move to Frankfurt. But I would have been happy to do that. At least then we would all be together again.

I sensed that my father wasn't "all here," that part of him was elsewhere although he was as friendly and affectionate as ever. He had things to do in the city, he said, but that didn't explain his absentmindedness. Hedda was a part of the conspiracy of silence around me, and I didn't dare to ask any questions for fear of upsetting whatever might still be left.

Finally my father was running out of time. I sensed how impatient he was getting, even if he didn't show it openly. He had to return to his job. One morning I woke up and looking out of the window saw that the fog had vanished, as if blown away, and the sun was shining from a cloudless, blue October sky. That day was like a bad dream: My father left by plane that same morning, and in the evening my mother landed at Tempelhof. I cried and cried and couldn't stop.

Not until my father was gone did I realize that something must have happened. I had to find out the truth no matter how painful, no matter what it might be. For the first time in my life, I decided I would no longer be satisfied with some threadbare explanation. I insisted on a believable answer. Why had father come to Berlin? What was it he had to do here. What was the real reason he came? If it was really just his work that kept him away, why didn't we just move to where he was? Finally my mother came out with the truth. She told me that they were getting a divorce. My father would not be living with us anymore, neither in Berlin nor in Frankfurt.

At that time I still hadn't heard anything about his plans to emigrate though.

The fog hanging over Berlin had prevented my parents from saying good-bye to each other before father left Europe. The personal drama of these two people who had once lived happily together, and who had stayed together so steadfastly through all those terrible years and had together withstood all pressures, actually grew out of their enforced geographical separation. Both had needed a trusted friend at their side, and had found other partners. And both were forced to admit that they could not longer resume their marriage, since it had slipped away from them several years before, during the war.

From talking with my mother and from the later letters written to her by my father, which I found only after her death, I concluded that both never quite got over being parted from each other.

A few months after his visit to Berlin, my father invited me to come to Hamburg. We spent three wonderful days there during which he showed me the city of his youth. We did the traditional harbor round-trip; we went to the theater and the movies. I still remember clearly that they were showing *Die Kinder des Olymp* (Children of Paradise). I felt unaccustomedly grown up and fully accepted. After this exciting excursion into the Big World I found the return to my everyday school life rather bland.

I complained to my mother about my everyday Berlin life not being anything like the marvelous days I had spent with my father in Hamburg. My reproaches to my mother earned me severe rebukes from my sister and Hedda, and an especially tough one from my Grandmother Zazi who had come for a visit from Zurich. They all came to mother's defense – justifiably – and said negative things about my father. I withdrew into my shell again.

But in spite of all the sermons, I still wasn't told anything about his emigration.

The shock I had a few months later when I received a letter from my father was that much worse. He wrote me that he had married Sylvia – formerly Tosia – the young woman from Drohobycz whom I'd met in Müggenburg, and that he was going to emigrate with her to America, "to that great, big, free country." I think by the time the letter reached me he was already on the ship to New York.

Over the years I didn't receive a single letter from my father in which he wasn't singing the praises of American freedom and liberty. I wasn't much interested in that; I'd much rather have heard from him that he missed his daughter, her siblings, life with us. When my mother asked, "What did he write you?" I rolled my eyes and said, "Well you know, about the wonderful freedom, as usual."

At first my father went to Virginia as caretaker on a farm there. But he couldn't stand the climate or the hard work. From there he moved to New York, where he and Sylvia more or less managed to get along. At that time, in the fifties, old friends of his who knew him from before talked quite frankly about the fact that he wasn't doing well. And Irene Feit later succinctly told me that he was very poor at that time. I think all his former strength was just used up. He never really rebounded. His old friend and comrade-in-arms Backenroth/Bronicki said in the interview I mentioned earlier, "Had he stayed in Germany – and atoned for the Nazi crimes that he didn't commit – instead of going to the USA and living modestly there, I'm convinced that he would long ago have held a high position in the Adenauer government."

I doubt that this could ever have been an alternative for him. He couldn't stand Germany any longer; it had broken him.

Donata and Eberhard were two very different people, in temperament and disposition. But I think the things they experienced, witnessed, and lived through during the war were so very different in each case, and their later lives continued to be influenced by this difference.

At any event, Donata's life took a much more positive turn than that of her former husband. Also there's no doubt that the enormous courage and energy that never let her down, determined the course of her life. After years of struggling to care for her family and find a way of supporting them, she succeeded – through a lucky coincidence and her own talent – in becoming a conference interpreter and traveling all over the world. She also worked for the Bonn government, with the result that in the mid-1950s she was offered a permanent position with the Language Services Department of the Foreign Ministry. Yet she turned down this offer, which to a woman in her mid-fifties without a pension, must have seemed like hitting the jackpot. "Too many old Nazis!" she said, casually naming some of them. No, the price was too high. She didn't want to have anything to do with those people ever again.

This recklessly self-assured decision didn't hurt her career. For more than twenty years she successfully continued her work as a freelance interpreter. She loved her profession very much, and considered this late career and the new horizons it presented as a great stroke of good fortune. Which indeed it was.

39

In addition to the prevailing lack of interest in confronting and talking about the recent past, there was also a decided indifference toward citizens of "the other Germany." Although it was precisely the directness and the human decency they had shown that could have destined them to help build up a civilized, democratic society. Therefore, it was not to be taken for granted when Joachim Lipschitz, Minister of the Interior of West Berlin, initiated a program in 1958 to honor citizens of Berlin who had helped victims of Nazi persecution during the NS regime. The story behind this initiative is quite interesting. For one thing, Lipschitz was himself "half-Jewish" by Nazi criteria and was not one of those who tried to repress mention of the recent past. Coincidentally, shortly before this Heinz Galinski, Chairman of the Berlin Jewish Community, had created the "Heinrich Stahl Prize" with the same intention. (It was named for the last Chairman of the Berlin Jewish Community. He had been deported to Theresienstadt in June 1942 at the age of 74, where he died five months later, allegedly from pneumonia.) In 1958, Galinski awarded the prize to nineteen Berlin citizens. Thirty-four years after this event, in April 1992, my sisters and I accepted this prize from Heinz Galinski, awarded to our parents posthumously. It was to be the last of these prizes he awarded, and the only prize that was jointly dedicated to Donata and Eberhard Helmrich.

In 1958 Joachim Lipschitz went to work. A large number of files were collected at the Berlin Restitution Office. More than one and a half thousand applications were processed; the Senate awarded the prize to seven hundred and fifty Berliners – of course only in the Western Sector of the city. The prerequisite was that

Donata Helmrich, in her Sylt home, 1965

the help was given often and altruistically – without any financial remuneration, and that the rescuers were endangering their own lives. If the rescuers were in need, there was a small additional monetary award as well. There was one restriction that can be explained by the prudery of those times: Prostitutes and petty criminals who had been rescuers – incidentally there were quite a few of these – were not deemed worthy of the distinction and were rejected as being *"ehrenrührig"* ("not honorable").

The Berlin list of names was to be the only one of its kind. Although the Senator had tried to induce other states in the Federal Republic to follow the Berlin example, he did not succeed. After Joachim Lipschitz died in 1961, his successor continued awarding the honors for a few more years. Eventually the program was terminated.

On July 17, 1962, Dr. Walter Schwarz, a lawyer from Berlin submitted a request to the Senate in which he pointed to "the meritorious acts by the married couple Helmrich during the NS period." In the answer he received, he was informed that Eberhard Helmrich, unfortunately, was not eligible "because he resided in New York and could therefore not be considered." But they would check to see "whether Donata Helmrich could be included in the honor." And that actually happened very quickly, for on August 2 she received an official written communication asking her to come to the Documentation Office, Room 331 on August 10, 1962 at 11 a.m. – bringing along her identity card – for a personal consultation.

I was able to examine my mother's file and I found in it many names I knew from my childhood or from stories she had told. How long ago it all was! I also found touching letters from survivors that vividly describe Donata's courage and readiness to help.

Among the papers there's also a copy of a document that was presented to her on the occasion of a memorial observance held in the hall the of the Jewish Congregation in Berlin Charlottenburg commemorating the twenty-second anniversary of the 1943 Uprising in the Warsaw Ghetto.

It says:

The Senate of Berlin herewith expresses
to Mrs.Donata Helmrich
its gratitude and acknowledgement of the help and shelter
she provided to those persecuted during the National
Socialist Dictatorship without regard for her own safety.
Berlin, April 20, 1965

The document is signed by the then-mayor Willy Brandt and by the Senator Responsible for Domestic Affairs Theuner.

Unfortunately the original of the document can no longer be found. It apparently vanished at some point. I wasn't particularly surprised at that, for although my mother was no doubt very happy with the recognition, she probably didn't think it was a very big thing. That's just like her!

Joachim Lipschitz gave his initiative the name: "Unsung Heroes." No doubt he was inspired by a book that Kurt R. Grossmann, who had emigrated from Germany to the USA, had published in New York in 1956. It came out in a German edition a year later, and the title was: *Die unbesungenen Helden: Menschen in Deutschlands dunklen Tagen (The Unsung Heroes: People in Germany's Dark Days)*.

This same Kurt Grossmann also "discovered" my father and wrote about him in his book. He became aware of him "through a coincidence," he wrote, "for he shied away from the spotlight." There is no doubt that Grossmann was in part responsible for the fact that toward the end of the sixties the Federal Government and the President began to decorate a relatively small number of rescuers with the *Bundesverdienstkreuz*. (So far there have been no more than about two hundred fifty.)

One of the first five award ceremonies, which took place in Beethoven Hall in Bonn on the Day of Prayer and Repentance in 1967, was for Eberhard Helmrich. However, he couldn't come from New York to take part in the ceremony.

The gala event was well attended. Groups of former resistance people from all over Germany had come, but what was supposed to be only the first in a series was soon forgotten again. Federal Minister Carolo Schmid and the Israeli Ambassador Asher Ben-Natan both presented exalted speeches, and Kurt Grossman recited a somewhat pompous poem by Alfred Kerr dedicated to the rescuers:

"The world hardly knows their names.

They glide along, dark and bright,
You take your hat off
To salute them a thousand times – but they don't see it.
They march and glide on; storms rage,
Some are caught; they are gone from this life;
But the league of the nameless lives on,
The invisible army of helpers.
Torture threatens, the torment is grim –
The fight goes on undeterred.
They are the saints and the knights
Of the human kingdom that is coming."

Yad Vashem sent a telegram on the occasion: "We hope with full hearts that these Righteous of the Nations shall become heroes of the German People."

Nothing came of that. The recipients of the awards certainly didn't want to be turned into heroes or saints! But they would surely have been in agreement with setting up a kind of guiding principle for the next generation.

40

When Eberhard Helmrich was awarded the *Bundesdienstkreuz* he had been living in the USA for almost eighteen years. He and his wife still kept in touch with a few people they knew from Germany and Poland, some of whom I mentioned previously. Their friends Irene and Michael Feit were the ones who accidentally heard a radio broadcast which mentioned the Israeli Memorial. The radio station was supporting its activities and urged listeners who knew of any rescuers to send in their names. This inspired Irene and Michael, and they began writing letters and telephoning across half the world, trying to find other people rescued by Eberhard Helmrich. And they all got together and sent an application to Yad Vashem asking that he be recognized as a "Righteous Among the Nations"

In 1965 this honor was conferred on Eberhard Helmrich and in July 1966 he received the medal and a document from the Israeli General Consul in New York. With that he also had the right to plant a tree on the Avenue of the Righteous.

I looked at the documents in Jerusalem – there are many letters archived, some in English, some in French or Polish, and some even in Hebrew. There is a long list of names in Hebrew and a thick packet of postcards with Israeli postmarks. Of course, I couldn't read them all, but a staff member of the Memorial told me that they were all registering for my father's award ceremony. They hadn't forgotten him after all.

At first my father couldn't even consider a flight to Israel, for that was not within his financial possibilities. But Irene and Michael Feit thought of a way around that. They started a collection. When they had collected enough money, they bought

From left to right: Irene Chalpin, Harvey Samo, Eberhard Helmrich, Eva Samo, presenting the flight ticket to Israel, New York 1966 | SICKLES Photo-Reporting, Maplewood, New Jersey

two plane tickets and gave them to Eberhard and his wife, making a little celebration out of it. They met at Lou Siegel's restaurant where to Eberhard's surprise no fewer than thirty people who owed him their lives had gathered.

I wonder how my father felt. Being in the limelight, as Kurt Grossmann had correctly remarked, was not his thing – and certainly public speaking wasn't. My poor father! For there was nothing for him now but to speak in public, to make speeches – when he was handed the plane tickets, at a meeting that the Jewish Agency had organized in his honor, and to the press.

It's obvious how hard that was for him from the copy of a speech (in English). Although it was typed, it is so full of Eberhard's handwritten additions and corrections that I had trouble deciphering it. In it he tells about his family, about

Eberhard Helmrich in Israel, March 1968

Germany, what it was like before Hitler came, and of his country's dramatic descent into barbarity. He talks less about himself than about those close to him. About his driver Wojnek he wrote: "You see, this man did more than I did. I, as a German, had a bad conscience, but he, as a Pole, was in a completely different situation." At the end of the manuscript he asks the question that he probably had often asked himself, but that kept being raised by others as well: How could he have endured that time? "When I look back," he writes, "then I can only say that a great deal of non-conformism was essential for the task I was given. It is relatively

Eberhard Helmrich in Israel, March 1968

easy to resist an enemy from the outside because you have the sympathy of your own people on your side. But to oppose the general, habitual way of thinking, the attitudes, and beliefs of your own people for almost thirteen years, that's something completely different. The price you have to pay is complete isolation. And sometimes I think I'm still paying for it."

In May 1967 Sylvia and Eberhard started their journey to plant his tree. They wanted to stop off in Europe first and then continue on to Israel. Unexpectedly, they hand to change their itinerary, for the Six-Day War had broken out. So their journey to the Land of the Covenant was postponed to the following year. They made visits instead – it took longer than planned – to various cities in Germany and other countries in Europe.

For Eberhard there was also a return to Berlin, to see Donata and me. During that time Sylvia stayed with friends in Frankfurt. It proved to be an almost hopeless task to take up a conversation after so many years. Where was one to start? At least I was glad on that occasion to introduce my father to his two grandchildren, one six and the other eight years old. It was a sad reunion, and my mother, who never cried, had tears in her eyes and her voice was full of melancholy.

In April 1968, Eberhard flew to Israel by himself. The newspaper *Welt am Sonntag* wrote: "Hundreds of people were at the Tel Aviv Airport to welcome Helmrich; they embraced him and thanked him." Eberhard was overcome by the warm reception; he didn't believe that so many people would come.

As a farewell present they gave him a little book that they had made for him. They had pasted photographs in it, including the latest ones taken at the tree planting, and written their own stories as well as the story of his many helpful activities. On the first page is a portrait photo of my father; below in beautiful handwriting, a moving poem in German:

ER
Wir bilden eine geschlossene Schar
Von traurigen, düsteren, trüben Gestalten,
Die kraftlos und – leider – jeder Freude bar
Sich krampfhaft der Erde erhalten.
Atemlos harren wir:
Unbekannt – das Ziel.
Durchhalten – der Sinn
Erleben – das Wort.
Allem zum Trotz – erleben.
Da stand er vor uns – schlank und hell,
Wir lauschten. Er hiess uns nicht verzagen.
Er lächelte – und war doch sehr traurig:
Er schwieg. Wir auch. Weshalb? Wir wussten es nicht.
Doch wie sollten wire es ihm sagen?
"Wir danken dir, dass du Mensch bist?"

Eberhard Helmrich, Christmas 1968, New York

HE

We form a solid company
Of somber, drab, and gloomy figures,
Who – weak and sadly bereft of any joy,
Maintain themselves on earth.
Breathlessly we wait:
Unknown – the goal.
Staying the course – the reason.
To live – the word,
In defiance of all – to live.
There he stood before us, slender and radiant,
We listened. He told us not to lose hope.
He smiled – and still was very sad:
He was silent. We were too. Why? We did not know.
Yet how were we to say it?
"We thank you for being a man, a Mensch"?

As soon as he was back in New York, Eberhard wrote to Donata: "I met more Drohobyczers than I expected; I planted my little tree. Travelled around the country, and saw a lot in two weeks. Probably not the real Israel, since during my stay there, everything was green and in bloom. All the hills were green and colorful with little flowers all over. The roses and hibiscus were in bloom; the air was sunny but moderately warm. Four weeks later everything will begin to turn brown and it stays that way into October. It is a very interesting country. In part very beautiful – but you know, Donaxchen, olive trees and citrus don't create a lovely landscape the way we picture it with deciduous trees." Was he homesick?

In another letter to her he recalls Keitum where by now Donata had established her "grandchildren central" and congratulated her. He wished he could see her again. It remained no more than a wish. In March 1969, he wrote her: "I'm getting fed up with the USA." The only thing that kept him there was the fact "that after many long years we are earning enough to be able to set aside some money for the future, which is absolutely essential. As long as I have this job and can work, I have to stick with it." By now he was sixty-nine years old.

It was his last letter. Two months later, on May 5th, he died of cancer that had been discovered too late.

A few days after his death there was a moving memorial service that I found out about only years later. Kurt Grossmann wrote about it in the *Jüdische Allgemeine*: "...but certainly the greatest honor was one he didn't live to see: the deeply emotional tribute by four hundred Americans – Black and White, professors, businessmen, and workers – one warm Sunday afternoon in New York, and the tears they shed for this extraordinary man." How much I would have liked to have been there.

Eberhard Helmrich's name turned up one other time in public. The matter was somewhat unusual. Reports even reached the German newspapers.

In the spring of 1985 the American President Ronald Reagan came to the Federal Republic of Germany, and among other events on his schedule was a visit together with Chancellor Helmut Kohl to the Military Cemetery in Bitburg. A hefty controversy had erupted about this plan because members of the Waffen SS were also buried there. At the same time there was a meeting in Jerusalem of twenty-five mayors from various countries, including five from Germany. They were scheduled among other things to make a trip to Yad Vashem, and it was planned to take this opportunity to signal their opposition to the visit to Bitburg by President Reagan. So the mayors gathered about Helmrich's tree; one man made a speech, and each of the people there put down a white rose.

41

Whether it was the newspaper stories about the white roses that that provided the impetus, or whether it had been a plan that was already in existence for some time, Mr. and Mrs. Samo from New Jersey became convinced that Donata had earned a tree of her own in Jerusalem. The idea that she wasn't to be considered because there was now another, a post-war Mrs. Helmrich, was in direct contradiction to their sense of justice.

They went to work and started looking for people who had known Donata, who owed their lives to her, and who were ready to support an application to the Israeli Memorial with their names and the stories of their rescues. They looked especially for women who had found shelter at the Westend Allee house. The response was positive. In a notarized letter Harvey Samo wrote to Jerusalem: "Over the years I have met a series of people who owe their lives to this woman. When I spoke to Donata Helmrich recently and informed her about our initiative and explained to her that we were nominating her for the 'Medal for the Righteous,' she replied, 'I only did what I considered right.' Mr. Eberhard Helmrich has been honored, and Mrs. Donata Helmrich who shared in many of his activities and above all who always shared with him the full risk of these actions, deserves equal recognition."

At the time Eva and Harvey Samo had asked Donata also to give them names of those she had helped. My mother wasn't well, but she did take a piece of paper and in a shaky hand wrote down several names and addresses. Below the list she had written with another pen, perhaps on another day, as if she had thought some more about it: "Eberhard actually did it all." In a letter of Eberhard's

Donata Helmrich, August 1983

to Donata, he seems to be pointing to a parallel: "I know that there is no doubt that you had a greater influence on the upbringing of the children than I did, but among the many successful things in my life, I always thought one of the best was having contributed, in a time of an overwhelming dictatorship, to four children being able to grow up in a human and free atmosphere."

I was often asked how many people survived thanks to the help of my parents. It may be surprising, but I can't really say. Because nobody can really say, and because "rescue" can't be defined simply. There are sources that mention seventy, others say "around a hundred individuals," and still others speak of two hundred and fifty; frequently the number three hundred is mentioned. It seems pointless to me to try to investigate this, to clear it up. The wisdom of the Talmud, the wisdom of the inscription on the medal that Yad Vashem awards to the rescuers applies here: Who saves one life, saves the whole world.

In August 1986 the Samoses received a letter from Jerusalem. In it they are informed that the commission that decides about awarding the honors has approved the award for Donata Helmrich. This gives her personally or a relative the right to plant a tree on the Avenue of the Righteous. The Israeli Embassy in Bonn would shortly be notified as well.

Our mother had died four months before this news arrived. My sisters and brother agreed that I should be the one to go to Israel to represent all of us. So eight months later, in April 1987, my youngest son Tilo and I flew to Tel Aviv. And from there we drove toward the hills of Judea to the Holy City.

On this trip we became part of a deeply moving, very precious piece of our family history. Since then it has been a deeply consoling thought for me that both Donata and Eberhard were memorialized in the same place.

Whenever I am in Israel, I visit the two trees. I break off some little twigs to bring back to my siblings and my children in Germany. Some with the strong, ovoid, dark green leaves of our father's large carob tree and some with delicate, elongated, silvery green leaves from our mother's olive tree.

Dr. Mordecai Paldiel, Director of the section "The Rightious among the Nations," in Yad Vashem, Jerusalem, Handing the little olive tree for Donata Helmrich to her daughter Cornelia, April 1987

Donata's olive tree in May 2001

Cornelia Schmalz-Jacobsen, planting
the olive tree for her mother, April 1987

Eberhard's Carob tree, Yad Vashem,
May 2001

223

YAD VASHEM
Har Hazikaron
Jérusalem

בזכירה
סוד הגאולה
(הבעש"ט)

DANS LE SOUVENIR
RÉSIDE LE SECRET
DE LA RÉDEMPTION
Baal Chem Tov

יד ושם
הר הזיכרון
ירושלים

תעודה

ATTESTATION

EBERHARD HELMRICH

ששׂ נמשׁו בכפי להצלת יהודים בתקופת השואה

QUI, AU PÉRIL DE sa VIE, a SAUVÉ DES JUIFS PENDANT
L'ÉPOQUE D'EXTERMINATION

נטע   עץ בשדרת חסידי אומות העולם

a   PLANTÉ UN ARBRE DANS L'ALLÉE DES JUSTES

LE 19
18 mars 1968

ביום י"ח אדר תשכ"ח

בשם רשות הזיכרון יד ושם
POUR L'INSTITUT DU SOUVENIR YAD VASHEM

בשם הוועדה לציון חסידי אומות השלם
POUR LA COMMISSION DES JUSTES

ונתתי להם יד ושם אשר לא יכרת ..... ישעיהו

"JE LEUR DONNERAI UN NOM ÉTERNEL, QUI NE PÉRIRA PAS" ISAIE, 56

Attestation from Yad Vashem for Eberhard, March 1968

YAD VASHEM
THE HOLOCAUST MARTYRS' AND HEROES'
REMEMBRANCE AUTHORITY
HAR HAZIKARON, JERUSALEM

ידושם
רשות הזיכרון
לשואה ולגבורה
הר הזיכרון, ירושלים

תעודה
ATTESTATION

Donata Helmrich

שמ"ה נפשה בכפה להצלת יהודים בתקופת השואה.

AU PERIL DE SA VIE A SAUVE DES JUIFS PENDANT L'HOLOCAUSTE

נטעה עץ בשדרת חסידי אומות העולם

A PLANTE UN ARBRE DANS L'ALLEE DES JUSTES

LE 24 Avril 1987   ביום כה ניסן תשמ"ז

Dr. Y Arad   בשם ועדה לצידו חסידי אומות העולם
בשם רשות הזיכרון יד-ושם   Pour la Commission des Justes
Pour l'Institut du Souvenir Yad Vashem

...ונתתי להם בביתי ובחומותי יד ושם... אשר לא יכרת. ישעיהו נ"ו

...JE LEUR DONNERAI UNE PLACE ET UN NOM...QUI NE PERIRA PAS...   ESAIE, 56

Attestation from Yad Vashem for Donata Helmrich, April 1987

225

About the author

Cornelia Schmalz-Jacobsen was born in Berlin. She has been a journalist and was active in politics; for many years she was a member of the FDP (Free Democratic Party) and has served in many official capacities. She has been Munich City Councilor, Berlin Senator, Member of the German Bundestag and Federal Commissioner for Foreign Nationals. She lives as a freelance writer in Berlin and is involved in an honorary capacity in various National and International Humanitarian Organizations.

Acknowledgements

I would like to thank all those who were willing to share with me their experiences and recollections in many long conversations. My special gratitude goes to Dr. Beate Kosmala and Dr. Claudia Schoppmann, at the time with the Center for Research on Anti-Semitism, to day on the staff of the Gedenkstätte Stille Helden (Memorial to Silent Heroes) in Berlin. Without Eva and Harvey Samo, who through many years collected material about both my parents and kept urging and encouraging me to work on this project, this story would never have been written.

Sources and Literature

Ruth Andreas-Friedrich, Der Schattenmann. Tagebuchaufzeichnungen 1939-1945, Berlin 1947.

Margret Boveri, Tage des Überlebens. Berlin 1945, Munich 1968.

Wolf Gruner, Judenverfolgung in Berlin 1933-1945. Eine Chronologie der Behördenmassnahmen in der Reichshauptstadt, 2 vollst. Überarb. Und stark erw. Aufl., Berlin 2009.

Wolf Gruner, Die Fabrik-Aktion und die Ereignisse in der Berliner Rosenstrasse: Fakten und Fiktionen um den 27. Februar 1943, in: Jahrbuch für Antisemitismus-forschung 11 (2002), S. 137-177.

Beate Kosmala/Claudia Schoppmann (Hrsg.), Solidarität und Hilfe für Juden während der NS-Zeit, Band 5: Überleben im Untergrund. Hilfe und Rettung für Juden in Deutschland 1941-1945, Berlin 2002.

Dieter Pohl, Nationalsozialistische Judenverfolgung in Ostgalizien 1941-1944. Organisation und Durchführung eines staatlichen Massenverbrechens, Munich 1997.

Dennis Riffel, Unbesungene Helden. Die Ehrungsinitiative des Berliner Senats 1958 bis 1966, Berlin 2007.

Thomas Sandkühler, "Endlösung" in Galizien. Der Judenmord in Ostpolen und die Rettungsinitiativen von Berthold Beitz 1941 bis 1944, Bonn 1996.

Joseph Walk, Das Sonderrecht für die Juden im NS-Staat. Eine Sammlung der gesetzlichen Massnahmen und Richtlinien, Heidelbert 1981.

Yad Vashem, Department "Righteous Among the Nations."

Federal Archive Koblenz.

State Archive of Berlin, section "Unbesungene Helden" (Unsung Heroes).

Central Archives of Ukraine.

Center for Anti-Semitic Research, Technical University Berlin, Archives.